Residual Figuration in Samuel Beckett and Alberto Giacometti

LEGENDA

LEGENDA is the Modern Humanities Research Association's book imprint for new research in the Humanities. Founded in 1995 by Malcolm Bowie and others within the University of Oxford, Legenda has always been a collaborative publishing enterprise, directly governed by scholars. The Modern Humanities Research Association (MHRA) joined this collaboration in 1998, became half-owner in 2004, in partnership with Maney Publishing and then Routledge, and has since 2016 been sole owner. Titles range from medieval texts to contemporary cinema and form a widely comparative view of the modern humanities, including works on Arabic, Catalan, English, French, German, Greek, Italian, Portuguese, Russian, Spanish, and Yiddish literature. Editorial boards and committees of more than 60 leading academic specialists work in collaboration with bodies such as the Society for French Studies, the British Comparative Literature Association and the Association of Hispanists of Great Britain & Ireland.

The MHRA encourages and promotes advanced study and research in the field of the modern humanities, especially modern European languages and literature, including English, and also cinema. It aims to break down the barriers between scholars working in different disciplines and to maintain the unity of humanistic scholarship. The Association fulfils this purpose through the publication of journals, bibliographies, monographs, critical editions, and the MHRA Style Guide, and by making grants in support of research. Membership is open to all who work in the Humanities, whether independent or in a University post, and the participation of younger colleagues entering the field is especially welcomed.

ALSO PUBLISHED BY THE ASSOCIATION

Critical Texts
Tudor and Stuart Translations • *New Translations* • *European Translations*
MHRA Library of Medieval Welsh Literature

MHRA Bibliographies
Publications of the Modern Humanities Research Association

The Annual Bibliography of English Language & Literature
Austrian Studies
Modern Language Review
Portuguese Studies
The Slavonic and East European Review
Working Papers in the Humanities
The Yearbook of English Studies

www.mhra.org.uk
www.legendabooks.com

STUDIES IN COMPARATIVE LITERATURE

Studies in Comparative Literature are produced in close collaboration with the British Comparative Literature Association, and range widely across comparative and theoretical topics in literary and translation studies, accommodating research at the interface between different artistic media and between the humanities and the sciences.

ALSO PUBLISHED IN THIS SERIES

20. *Aestheticism and the Philosophy of Death: Walter Pater and Post-Hegelianism*, by Giles Whiteley
21. *Blake, Lavater and Physiognomy*, by Sibylle Erle
22. *Rethinking the Concept of the Grotesque: Crashaw, Baudelaire, Magritte*, by Shun-Liang Chao
23. *The Art of Comparison: How Novels and Critics Compare*, by Catherine Brown
24. *Borges and Joyce: An Infinite Conversation*, by Patricia Novillo-Corvalán
25. *Prometheus in the Nineteenth Century: From Myth to Symbol*, by Caroline Corbeau-Parsons
26. *Architecture, Travellers and Writers: Constructing Histories of Perception*, by Anne Hultzsch
27. *Comparative Literature in Britain: National Identities, Transnational Dynamics 1800-2000*, by Joep Leerssen
28. *The Realist Author and Sympathetic Imagination*, by Sotirios Paraschas
29. *Iris Murdoch and Elias Canetti: Intellectual Allies*, by Elaine Morley
30. *Likenesses: Translation, Illustration, Interpretation*, by Matthew Reynolds
31. *Exile and Nomadism in French and Hispanic Women's Writing*, by Kate Averis
32. *Samuel Butler against the Professionals: Rethinking Lamarckism 1860–1900*, by David Gillott
33. *Byron, Shelley, and Goethe's Faust: An Epic Connection*, by Ben Hewitt
34. *Leopardi and Shelley: Discovery, Translation and Reception*, by Daniela Cerimonia
35. *Oscar Wilde and the Simulacrum: The Truth of Masks*, by Giles Whiteley
36. *The Modern Culture of Reginald Farrer: Landscape, Literature and Buddhism*, by Michael Charlesworth
37. *Translating Myth*, edited by Ben Pestell, Pietra Palazzolo and Leon Burnett
38. *Encounters with Albion: Britain and the British in Texts by Jewish Refugees from Nazism*, by Anthony Grenville
39. *The Rhetoric of Exile: Duress and the Imagining of Force*, by Vladimir Zorić
40. *From Puppet to Cyborg: Pinocchio's Posthuman Journey*, by Georgia Panteli
41. *Utopian Identities: A Cognitive Approach to Literary Competitions*, by Clementina Osti
43. *Sublime Conclusions: Last Man Narratives from Apocalypse to Death of God*, by Robert K. Weninger
44. *Arthur Symons: Poet, Critic, Vagabond*, edited by Elisa Bizzotto and Stefano Evangelista
45. *Scenographies of Perception: Sensuousness in Hegel, Novalis, Rilke, and Proust*, by Christian Jany
46. *Reflections in the Library: Selected Literary Essays 1926–1944*, by Antal Szerb
47. *Depicting the Divine: Mikhail Bulgakov and Thomas Mann*, by Olga G. Voronina
48. *Samuel Butler and the Science of the Mind: Evolution, Heredity and Unconscious Memory*, by Cristiano Turbil
49. *Death Sentences: Literature and State Killing*, edited by Birte Christ and Ève Morisi
50. *Words Like Fire: Prophecy and Apocalypse in Apollinaire, Marinetti and Pound*, by James P. Leveque

Residual Figuration in Samuel Beckett and Alberto Giacometti

Lin Li

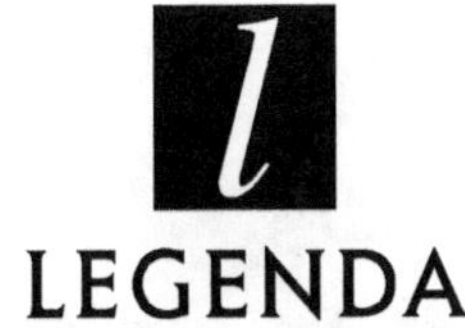

LEGENDA
Studies in Comparative Literature 53
Modern Humanities Research Association
2022

Published by Legenda
an imprint of the Modern Humanities Research Association
Salisbury House, Station Road, Cambridge CB1 2LA

ISBN 978-1-78188-662-5 (HB)
ISBN 978-1-78188-666-3 (PB)

First published 2022

Copy-Editor: Charlotte Brown

CONTENTS

ACKNOWLEDGEMENTS

This book is the product of my PhD at Cambridge, and I would like to thank many individuals for their support throughout these years: Timothy Mathews for believing in me, Sascha Bru for pushing me on, Brandon Yen and Peter Dale for silently supporting me from Essex, James Cetkovski for being there, my families in Belgium and Singapore for putting up with me, and Stijn, Anna and Clara Conix for loving me.

I'm grateful to the following for financial support: the MDRN team at KU Leuven, The International Society for the Study of Narrative, and the Textbook and Academic Authors Association.

Lastly, I'd like to thank everyone at MHRA Legenda for seeing this project through, especially Charlotte Brown, Graham Nelson, Emily Finer and Wen-Chin Ouyang. I'd also like to thank David Jones for his extremely helpful comments on earlier drafts of this book.

INTRODUCTION

ESTRAGON: I tell you we weren't here yesterday. Another of your nightmares.

VLADIMIR: And where were we yesterday evening according to you?

ESTRAGON: How do I know? In another compartment. There's no lack of void.

SAMUEL BECKETT, *Waiting for Godot*[1]

I must paint the void in front of me. The void begins at the tip of the nose.

ALBERTO GIACOMETTI to Isaku Yanaihara[2]

I first encountered Beckett as an undergraduate at the National University of Singapore on a foundational English Literature module. Funnily enough, what first struck me so vividly about Beckett did not come about through a direct encounter with his works or a lecture on them. Instead, my lecturer had slipped in Beckett's line as a joke just as he released us for a break: 'Let's convene later, no matter how difficult these texts are, or how boring my teaching is. After all, as Beckett's Unnamable said, "I can't go on, I will go on." So we will.'[3] That afternoon, something about the symmetry, precision and solidarity of those words struck a deep chord in me; the words were musical, exact and moving. I wondered about the kind of character behind those lines and dashed off to the library to borrow *The Unnamable*. (No character to be found.) Four years later, while working on my thesis on Beckett's poetry in the library of the same university, I stumbled upon Timothy Mathews's 'Walking with Angels in Giacometti and Beckett' and encountered Giacometti's figures for the first time. I remember being struck by the same sense of connection and desolation that I had felt in that English Literature 101 classroom; these figures seemed to have walked out of Beckett's pages. I was drawn to how both Beckett's and Giacometti's figures, seemingly abstract and impenetrable, simultaneously harboured the tireless, precise and laborious marks of each artist's artistic practices. I thought it was this liminality between the mute and the voiced, the static and the mobile, that gave their figures a common language: the language of a figure's coming-to-be, of figuration, that appeared to be even more powerful, and resonant, and uncertain, when both artists were read against each other. I found it very surprising that I — a Singaporean Chinese more at home with Singlish and the Nanyang style — might perceive an unwavering sense of connection with the works of Beckett and Giacometti across boundaries of contexts, histories, cultures and languages.

Thus, this book began as an investigation into this vaguely termed 'language of figuration' in Beckett's drama and Giacometti's art. I was interested in how this figuration was created and experienced differently in various media, and yet was brought together through a common reading that was partly performative and partly interpretive, visual and rhetorical, temporal and spatial. I quickly realized that my investigation into this mode of reading had to begin with an understanding of how the processes of depiction and perception worked together to create the human figures in these works. While these processes were very different in each medium, the resulting impression they gave was similar: human figures appeared to be made and un-made at the same time. This resulted in their appearing incomplete, unfinished and constantly in the process of becoming or returning to something else. It was this perpetual shifting between a figure and its figuration that made it hover between character and body, narrative and symbol.

The two men were no strangers to each other. They met in Paris in the mid-1930s and frequented the same cafes in Montparnasse. Even before they collaborated directly on the re-staging of *Waiting for Godot* in 1961, their works were frequently seen in Eugène Jolas's magazine *Transition*.[4] George Reavey, who introduced Beckett to the painters Bram and Geer van Velde, published Beckett's *Echo's Bones* in 1935 (Europa Press's first book) and had initially approached Giacometti to create its frontispiece.[5] To Beckett, Giacometti's art was 'granitically subtle, and all in inverted perceptions', but to Jean Genet, it was an art of 'superior tramps' — an echo of Beckett's early stage characters.[6]

That both Beckett's and Giacometti's figures appear fragmented, disembodied or residual is not a new point; indeed, images of Beckett's Mouth in *Not I*, May in *Footfalls* or the wraithlike column of Giacometti's *Femme Leoni* would encourage this comparison, even if scholarship had not already made it explicit.[7] Neither is it a new point that Beckett and Giacometti have in common subtractive artistic practices such as erasure, elimination and reduction.[8] Instead, what I aim to investigate is how these features are composed simultaneously through the depiction and perception of figures, and how this figural composition — broadly summarized above as the figure being made and un-made at the same time — possibly lends itself to new ways of thinking about the connections between human figures, figures of thought and figures of speech. In addition, the composition seems to bring the two artists closer through ways that are not confined to the historical or thematic; by deriving an understanding that remains honest to both the depiction and perception of the works, it surpasses a mere spotting of literary and visual characteristics or influences between them.

In order to give a sense of what is meant by a figure being made and un-made at the same time, and how this shifting between the figure and its figuration can serve as a basis for comparison between works of different media, I will first make a few comparative remarks on two of their works which exemplify the over-arching concerns of this book, namely Beckett's *Catastrophe* and Giacometti's sculpture installation, the *Chase Manhattan Project*.

'This craze for explicitation!'[9]

In 1982, Samuel Beckett wrote *Catastrophe* for then-imprisoned Czech playwright Václav Havel upon the invitation of the Association Internationale de Défense des Artistes (AIDA) for the Avignon Festival. The short play features four characters: D, the director, A, his female assistant, P, the protagonist, and L, Luke, who remains offstage and is in charge of the lighting. The play appears to represent a play in rehearsal; the main action and dialogue consist of D questioning and ordering A to adjust the posture and appearance of P, who stands mid-stage shivering on a black block, dressed in a black gown and black hat. D's comments reveal that his primary aim is for P's feet to be seen by the stalls but not the slightest 'trace of face' to be exposed, and his adjustments of P chiefly involve stripping him bare — he tells A that they 'could do with more nudity' — and whitening the 'cranium' and 'all flesh'.[10] The play ends with the light on P's head alone and the sound of distant applause, which falters and dies when P raises his head and fixes the audience. With that 'trace of face', P defies the dehumanized image of 'catastrophe' that D had aimed to stage, and inverts that controlled stasis upon the audience in their act of looking.[11] The face is powerful not only because it is shown but because it looks, and in looking demands to be looked back at. In that silent confrontation, the face 'wakes us to the theatricality that holds us in sway' and performs the stage;[12] it lays bare the gaze of the theatre and enacts its own looking back.[13]

P's face achieves an effect of theatre-reading by negating the processes of its elimination. But these processes of elimination are also those of creation; in staging the rehearsal of a play that aims to stage its catastrophe as a very precise image, *Catastrophe* emphasizes these processes of elimination as processes of work and production on the one hand, and violence and silence on the other. Yet, this unfolding — and here recalling the word 'catastrophe' from the Greek καταστροφή, a reversal or unravelling — does not result in neat and straightforward inversions of creation and elimination. It is not so much that *Catastrophe* gives a version of resistance as that it actually interrogates its processes of narrative-making. By this, I mean that *Catastrophe* provokes questions with regard to the focalization and framing of figures that represent and resist; the viewer, in being left with no straightforward position of identification, neither with the characters D or A, nor with the figure P, occupies an uneasy space as witness and participant in the theatrics of representation both in politics and art.[14]

One way of looking at how this space is created for the viewer is to trace how P the protagonist is depicted and perceived. Three main features characterize P. First, P is constantly being reduced, compressed or materialized — what appears at the start to be a shrouded human figure is gradually subtracted from until it becomes a made-to-fit staged image. By whitening him out, stripping him bare and eliminating any 'trace of face', P is erased of identity markers and flattened into a material semblance seemingly incapacitated from giving or receiving recognition, as the 'face' is usually required for both. Yet these processes of elimination are also emphasized as processes of production and creation; the narrative of erasure is simultaneously a work in progress. This palimpsestic mode of creating means that P is a figure constantly being made and un-made at the same time. This is characteristic of many of the figures that pervade Beckett's late dramatic works. Reader and Listener in *Ohio Impromptu*, for instance, seem to converge as one figure in the course of Reader's words gradually depicting, through its narrative, the visual image that is staged.[15] The static visual figures of Reader and Listener are filled in with verbal and textual figuration; the movement of figuration gives the impression of its catching up with, re-writing and pre-writing the visual figures into the verbal narrative of their '[growing] to be as one'.[16] However, this filling in of the figures with figuration — and here it can be compared, analogously, to the filling in of figure outlines with strokes and colours in a drawing — also pre-empts their knotting together towards silence with the 'sad tale a last time told' and their eventually '[turning] to stone'; in knocking for Reader's last line ('Nothing is left to tell') to be uttered again Listener at once struggles against this conflation and erasure of figure and figuration.[17]

Second, these processes of making and un-making P are made reflexive and explicit not only because the play is a rehearsal-in-progress, but because the audience's act of looking at P gradually aligns with that of D — especially after he exits the stage but continues giving commands — and, at the end of the play, supplants that of the imaginary audience for which the rehearsal is staged. The viewer becomes conscious of their active act of looking at the play — not just in relation to the staged text, but also to the actor and to other members of the audience — which reifies the play in its processes, structures and processions of performativity.[18] Perhaps nowhere is this seen more clearly in *Catastrophe* than at the end when the artificial applause subsides and P's face fades into the silent darkness: should the real audience now clap at the actual catastrophe of *Catastrophe*?[19] This making explicit of the gestures and processes of theatre-watching renders perceptible the formal depiction of drama, which moves the figure further into the processes of its figuration both within the creative process and the performance. In fact, this second characteristic of the figure P can be seen within the larger context of modernism and its tendencies. In *Beckett, Modernism and the Material Imagination*, Steven Connor writes that modernism is characterized in two ways: the first by 'expansion and experiment', and the second by 'finitude' or, in Peter Sloterdijk's term, 'explicitation'.[20] Connor further argues that the two characterizations work intricately; insofar as 'explicitation' is a deliberate and conscious articulation of processes previously left 'unconscious' or 'taken for granted', it furthers the first tendency of modernism to innovate and expand, but in doing so, necessarily returns modernism to its limits as it makes manifest 'forms of situation and limit'.[21]

Third, the figure P appears to eventually defy the 'catastrophe' it was made for and to supplant its reduced, dehumanized figure with its own remaining fragment of an illuminated, floating face. This face in looking and being looked back upon regains an instant of authorial presence which it had lost or indeed never really had throughout the play, but more than that, it exposes and emphasizes the audience's gaze as necessarily both part of and concealed in the process of making meaning in the theatre. It thus re-collects, recollects and exceeds P as figure by denying — or in some senses, negating — the processes of its creation. But because P's face is created through a process of making and un-making, and realized as a self-conscious effect of theatre-reading, it is a form of figure that while assertive, is highly temporal, elusive and ghost-like. This gives the impression of P still about to appear, or always on the brink of disappearing, or remaining after the light has faded. Such residual figures recur in many of Beckett's plays and especially in the late dramaticules such as *Rockaby* and *What Where*, where the gradation of light on the figure(s) in empty space likewise appears to be significant in establishing the sense of the remainder and the remaining.

Taking these three observations together, *Catastrophe* thus presents a figure P that appears to become its figuration or to extend from it an alternative figure; the final face that gazes at the audience is at once chillingly and hearteningly divorced from the passive, flattened image that it had been part of, and, in this final gesture of looking up, reinstates a kind of figural presence that straddles the physicality of the actor and the opening possibility of narration. In looking up, P makes us look back, realize our looking back, and question our looking at — it moves the very modes and precepts of representation, and because of that, cannot be comfortably nudged into the category of figure or figuration. This resulting entity is what I call 'residual figuration': it is a part of the figure and its figuration, but ultimately exceeds them and lends itself to the formulation of a gestural or rhetorical move from the work.

A similar approach can be taken to understand Giacometti's figures. As with most of Giacometti's works, what we now refer to as the *Chase Manhattan Project* has a convoluted history involving various versions, modifications, omissions and placements. In 1958, the architect Gordon Bunshaft approached Giacometti to make a public sculpture for the plaza in front of the new headquarters of the Chase Manhattan bank — a sixty-storey glass and steel tower — in New York City. Bunshaft's initial suggestion was to enlarge Giacometti's *Trois hommes qui marchent* [Three Walking Men] (1949), but Giacometti rejected it and came up with a new proposal comprising three figures: a walking man, a standing woman and a large head.[22] The project eventually fell through as Giacometti felt that none of the figures 'came right' and he had 'practically no feelings about how they should be grouped'.[23] In 1960, after making at least forty walking men, ten standing women and two large heads, he cast in bronze a total of seven versions of the three types of figures — *Grande Femme I, II, III* and *IV, L'Homme qui marche I* and *II*, and *Grande Tête* — and destroyed the rest.[24] These sculptures were then displayed in various combinations and spaces, such as for the Venice Biennale in 1962, in the Beyeler Foundation, in Basel, and in the courtyard of the Maeght Foundation, Saint-Paul de Vence, in 1964, where they still stand.

It is difficult to approach the *Chase Manhattan Project*. The different eye levels of the figures and their stark contrasts in frame give an impression of their inhabiting distinct implied spaces. This makes the exhibition space appear less neutral and more heterogeneous, and the viewer becomes more conscious of the different distances and angles involved in viewing each figure. All three figures appear to be highly stylized and striking even though they are perceived very differently at first glance. Of them, *Grande Femme* appears to be the most reduced, compressed and minimalistic. This is primarily a result of the differing impressions that a viewer gets from the profile and frontal views. From the side, it looks like an undifferentiated, vertical pillar with only a very vague indication of human features. This is a result of its towering height at 270 cm and the sheer geometric contrast between the fragile, vertical attenuation of the main frame and the clumpy, horizontal sedimentation at the base; the presence it asserts is of a two-dimensional flatness stencilled into its background. Depth is barely promised and the utter stasis of the object-figure is accentuated by a sense of anonymity resulting from the lack of differentiation in the contour, material mass and surface.

This is not the impression one gets from every tall Giacometti figure. For instance, *L'Homme qui marche* is easily recognizable as a human figure from all angles due to its stride, and *Grande Tête*, while definitely not belonging to the tall, skinny category, also asserts its human, though monumental, presence due to its thick, elongated neck and double stand. However, returning to *Grande Femme*, if one approaches the figure from its front rather than the side, the shape of a female figure is now recognizable, but it remains difficult to place it in perspective due to the extreme stylization of the figure, which throws off any sense of scaling. The overt stylization of the figure comes from its emaciation and elongation; it appears to have been trimmed off and stretched out at the same time. The waist, for instance, is almost as thin as the neck, and the distance between the bust and the hips is greatly exaggerated.

Bringing the profile and frontal views together, the figure is thus created by way of subtraction and addition, not just as material amalgamation of its creative processes, but also as an effect of being read from different positions of looking. The geometric contrast between its frame and its base comes across strongly when seen from the side, but the effect of elongation and emaciation is more pronounced when seen from the front; it is the mobility of the viewer in his or her various positions that composes and re-composes the figure in these different aspects of reduction and flattening. This highly material presence created by *Grande Femme* becomes at once assertive and extremely brittle — such an impression can also be seen in other female figures such as the *Femme debout* series of 1948–49, and the *Femmes de Venise* series of 1956, although they do not approach the scale of *Grande Femme.* Such a presence is no doubt intensified by the implied stasis of the female figure, which in Giacometti's post-surrealist sculptures is always standing or sitting.[25]

Grande Femme thus shares with P the same characteristics of being constantly reduced and compressed, except that the viewer here takes an active spatial role in participating and engaging with the making and un-making of the figure in its alternation between geometric flatness and linearity. Like P in *Catastrophe*, the figuration of *Grande Femme* is also palimpsestic: the marks of making the figure are superimposed on those that appear to erase or eliminate its excesses, and vice versa. This results in the making and the un-making of the figure being dependent on each other, which erodes the notion of a figure that can be clearly distinguished from its figuration.

What further intensifies this impression is that such processes of making and un-making become reflexive when traces or forms of depiction are left visible in the work or made increasingly present to the viewer in his or her experience of the work. In *Grande Femme*, the processes of figuration already seen in *Catastrophe*, are emphasized upon moving closer to the figure. Since the four female figures range from about 235 to 280 cm , most viewers will be confronted at eye level with a heavily worked over surface of bronze between the woman's waist and hips. The surface of the figure here is vivid, irregular and tactile. This is surprising because it contrasts with its apparently homogeneous, undifferentiated and elusive appearance from a distance, and defamiliarizes our everyday perceptions of bodies and representations of them in classical and modern art. What the viewer sees here are the cracks, protrusions and undulations of the bronze that emphasize the body as a surface of creating. As noted by Alex Potts, even though many other modernist sculptors have made human figures with highly textured surfaces, Giacometti's figures are unique in how the deep crevasses and knobbly irregularities of the body do not orientate a reading of the figure according to line and contour, in contrast to those of Rodin, for instance.[26] Here, the details of Giacometti's incessant working and re-working are left behind on and in the material as material; the marks and crevasses take away from the mass of the bronze as much as they define its contorted surface.

However, such material sedimentation of the creative process not only makes visible the artistic processes of making and subtracting, it also questions this position of extreme visibility that the viewer now has in relation to the sculpture. Has one perhaps stepped too close? The title of the art work, *Grande Femme*, tells the viewer what to look for and to figure out, and this step closer to the figure makes the viewer conscious of having lost or strayed from the optimal position from which to view the figure as it is so named. In this sense, the irregular surface of the body makes the viewer conscious of engaging in an active act of looking at the sculpture rather than a passive viewing of it; this destabilizes the viewer's spatial neutrality in relation to the figure and further nudges it into its figuration.

Lastly, and similarly to *Catastrophe*, it is the face that emphasizes the residual figuration of the figure of *Grande Femme*. If we were to look up at her from our hypothetical close-up position in the previous paragraph, what we see is neither elusiveness nor tangibility, but the marring of disfigurement. While it appeared previously that we might have stepped too close to the figure, in now looking up we see a face that while close, does not appear to be near; the proximity we share in space has no bearing on the proximity of intimacy and recognition. However, this is not to say that the face is always already too far away, because the crux of the issue here is the selectiveness of what is shown. We can see the precise marks that go into creating the very texture of the face, and yet we fail to garner from these details a human face that could be clearly identified as a person; here, as in *Catastrophe*, the categories of figure and character, human and person, are less straightforward.

I posit that this selectiveness of what is shown is a form of indexicality. In negating and making arbitrary our different positions of looking at the face in relation to establishing any form of proximal recognition with it — that is, one either sees it vaguely unclear from afar or clearly vague from up close — we are cued to read the face not as a visual component of a figure, but as a process of its making the figure show up. This means that the face projects the directionality of our reading: the disfigurement constantly points our looking elsewhere and negates any notion of a fully-perceived figure from an optimal position of perception. Thus, the disfigured face denies clear recognition of a human figure but points towards it, paradoxically, as a looking-away rather than looking-at. In this sense, it becomes a gesture for the figure that remains as a kind of inaccessible residue.

The three characterizations of P in *Catastrophe* and *Grande Femme* can here be summarized briefly. First, they are perceived to be constantly made and un-made due to a palimpsestic layering of figure production and figure subtraction; second, this making and un-making is further intensified by an increasing visibility and reflexivity of the forms and marks of depiction; and third, the interweaving of perception and depiction complicates notions of figure, figuration and character, resulting in an extension of a gestural or rhetorical figure characterized through a mode of reading that I call residual figuration.

When seen in the light of residual figuration, the figures of *Grande Femme* and *Catastrophe* become sites of reading. Instead of merely being objects to be interpreted, they *necessitate* a careful and honest negotiation with processes of withdrawal and disintegration, in both their depiction and our positions of perception. Further, residual figuration actively interrogates pre-conceived notions of figures and shows new extensions of figures; the disfigured face of *Grande Femme* becomes a gesture for the figure that is inaccessible, and the ghostly, gazing face of *Catastrophe* produces an effect of theatre-reading that asserts yet negates the presence of the figure in that instant of the audience's looking.

What residual figuration proposes are relations of figure-making within and between works of Beckett and Giacometti; taking this as the point of entry into inter-medial reading would allow further comparisons of how narration, narrativity and narratives are conceived in verbal and visual art. However, such a reading necessitates a grasp of how interactions of perception and depiction have been discussed in visual art and theatre works. One useful point of entry into this scholarship is through the concepts diegesis and deixis, from which can be extended the significance of relating spaces between the viewer/reader and the figures through processes of reading, looking and listening in different media.

Diegesis and Deixis

Broadly put, diegesis as understood in literature and theatre refers to an indirect mode of representation that is commonly aligned with a third-person narrative voice; this is opposed to mimesis, which is aligned with the direct mode of presenting a character by imitating the character's voice, behaviour and gestures.[27] In theatre works, diegesis frequently takes the form of diegetic speech spoken by a chorus or some form of narrating character, and in this capacity is able to interrupt the mimetic space of the stage either by projecting an alternative verbal version of the main action, or by referring back to the written dramatic text. In this very general sense, depiction and perception are interwoven via diegesis and mimesis, literature and theatre, text and performance. On the other hand, deixis as it is understood in the visual arts generally refers to elements in the artwork that refer back to the time, space and process of the creation.[28] These deictic references are usually aligned with reflexive painterly traces that are left unconcealed in the artwork and which, therefore, visibly emphasize the temporal and material processes of artistic creation. Just as deictic pronouns such as 'I' and 'you' point to a specific locus of utterance, deictic references in the art object refer to the specific spatio-temporal act of creation, hence bringing depiction into the perceived artwork.

These two concepts are very useful in understanding how depiction works its way back into perception and how both are eventually interwoven in the plays and the visual artworks, but they are also riddled with very complex and frequently contentious issues within their own fields. For a start, I would like to consider diegesis as presented by Martin Puchner in *Stage Fright: Modernism, Anti-theatricality, and Drama*, due to its explicit focus on how the concept troubles text and performance in modernist plays. Following that, I will examine deixis as presented in Norman Bryson's *Vision and Painting: The Logic of the Gaze*, as it gives a fundamental account of the semiotic term as applied to visual art, which other visual theorists such as Mieke Bal have acknowledged and from which they have developed their own thought.[29]

Puchner traces the distinction and the struggle between theatrical diegesis and mimesis to the anti-theatrical writings of Plato. In Book 3 of *The Republic*, Plato criticizes the figure of the actor — which he aligns with the Greek term ὑποκριτής — by contrasting verbal diegesis and theatrical mimesis through an early episode of the *Iliad* in which Chryses attempts to get Agamemnon to return his daughter. When the Homeric rhapsode changes from narrating the action in the third person to likening his voice and gesture to Chryses's in the first person, the rhapsode is seen to have switched from a 'pure and simple diegesis', or a 'diegesis without mimesis', to a 'diegesis through mimesis'.[30] This is 'fateful' because the poet now 'hides' under the mask of the character 'made out of a false voice and false gestures', and Plato in turn offers a translation of Chryses's speech into the third person.[31] The distinction between mimesis and diegesis, broadly characterized as imitation and narrative, thus forms the basis of Plato's anti-theatrical stance.

While Puchner goes on to give an illuminating account of how Aristotle plays down this distinction in order to defend mimesis, he ultimately insists that Plato's distinctions be held in order to examine precisely these anti-theatrical forces that are prevalent in modern theatre and drama.[32] He goes on to formulate diegesis as 'the indirect, descriptive or narrative representation of objects, persons, spaces and events through language (either spoken by a rhapsode, narrator, chorus, or author or represented in the dramatic text for the reader)' and theatrical mimesis as 'the direct representation of such objects, persons, speeches, spaces, and events on a stage'.[33] While Greek and Western drama have included numerous forms of diegesis such as chorus commentary or reported offstage action to enlarge the scope of representation beyond the stage, modernist diegesis differentiates itself by referring 'to the mimetic space of the stage itself'.[34] This diegesis can be 'written or printed diegesis' such as 'stage directions, descriptive and diegetic speech in closet drama' or 'performed diegesis' such as the 'diegetic speech spoken by a chorus' and they function as strategies to frame, control and interrupt the mimetic space.[35]

What is most useful about Puchner's framework is that it accommodates forms of theatrical diegesis implicated by the changing relations between the written dramatic text and the performance in modern theatre; this is evident in the case of, what Puchner terms, the 'modernist closet drama', which is an extreme case of a drama that 'seeks to interrupt and break apart any possibility for either an actual or an imaginary stage', and thus can only be realized in its reading.[36] Stage directions, for Puchner, take on a central role not just in closet drama but in a large part of modern drama, especially that of Beckett:

> All stage directions are descriptions or prescriptions of the mimetic space on the stage, but traditionally the doubling inherent in this projection disappears because stage directions are considered dispensable technical appendixes that do not appear in the end product, the performance. But when drama realizes itself as reading drama, its stage directions no longer disappear and thus suddenly take on new significance; they constitute a narrative or third-person discourse that takes over, for the reader, the mimetic space of the stage. [...] Reading the plays of Beckett requires a double reading of direct speech and stage directions, and his plays are therefore split between a theatre of dialogue and a theatre of objects and gestures, the latter captured by the descriptive diegesis of stage directions.[37]

Puchner effectively explicates this argument in his chapter on Beckett, paying special attention to three aspects of his plays: first, the erasure of the actor's gesture in favour of isolated, expressive gestures of habit such as in *Endgame*; second, the centrality of stage directions in plays such as *Act Without Words* and *Not I*; and third, the interruption of speech by gestures, which Puchner aligns with the interruption of reading by printed stage directions, in plays such as *Not I* and *Happy Days*.

Puchner's distinction between diegesis and mimesis is especially useful to understanding the depiction and perception of figures in Beckett's plays because it acknowledges the importation not only of the written dramatic text into theatre, but also the actual process of reading the text. The point is a refined one and valuable for understanding perception and depiction in the theatre, because it reveals that depiction and perception cannot be conveniently aligned with the creative process and the theatre performance respectively. For instance, in the above case of *Happy Days*, Puchner argues that the interruptive reading experience of the dramatic text — in which characters' spoken words are constantly interrupted by stage directions — is transposed onto the mimetic stage of the theatre itself through gestures that keep interrupting speech. Such gestures as Winnie's constant fanning and raising of her head are by themselves isolated, minor and habitual gestures, but because they are repeated and extracted from their contexts, they constitute, for Puchner, a 'set of constructed rules governing the play'.[38] This means that the mimetic constructs a new level of narrative; indeed, it is not so much that Winnie generates interruption as that she actually operates through it and as it. Winnie figures interruption; this progression is further intensified by her lines being increasingly riddled with interruptive figures of speech, a perceived effect rendered immediately visible in the graphic appearance of the dramatic text. Understanding interruption on several levels of mimesis and diegesis in *Happy Days* could, therefore, begin to explain Beckett's characterization of Winnie as 'an interrupted being'.[39]

In addition, Puchner's delineation provides very productive ways of understanding plays in which difficulties in hearing and seeing arise in the reader and the theatre audience to varying degrees. For instance, the whispered secrets of the women in *Come and Go* are unheard and unread by both the audience and the reader, while the lines spoken by the figures in *Play* are so rapid as to be incomprehensible to the audience yet clearly readable by the reader. In these cases, silence and the utter lack of silence become markers of intelligibility which cannot be clearly characterized as depicted text or perceived drama, but which, instead, derive from an intermingling of depiction and perception in the processes of reading texts and watching performances.

Puchner's modernist theatrical diegesis then, especially in the form of written diegetic strategies such as stage directions, forms an analogue to the concept of deixis in the visual arts. Deixis is a term from linguistics that is most easily understood through deictic markers such as 'I' and 'you' or 'here' and 'there',[40] which acquire meaning 'within a specific situation of utterance' and 'require a subject's presence'.[41] In Norman Bryson's formulation, deixis is aligned with painterly signs and forms that 'permit a maximum of integrity and visibility to the constitutive strokes of the brush'; this results in the import of the artistic process into the finished artwork both as a form of temporality in 'real time' and as an 'extension of the painter's own body'.[42] Thus, the deictic marker 'points' to the creative production of the artwork involving the artist and his or her locus of creation; it can be seen as a kind of index that 'signifies on the basis of an existential relationship of contiguity with its meaning', and which, Bal argues, can be aligned with Peircean indexicality.[43]

Bryson takes up deixis as a tool to contrast developments in Western and Chinese representational painting. The concealing of deixis in favour of an unobtrusive painted surface of realism in much of Western painting removes the duration and labour of creation, which Bryson equates with 'deictic time' and *durée:*

> Western painting is predicated on *the disavowal of deictic reference* [...]. The temporality of Western representational painting is rarely the deictic time of the painting as process; that time is usurped and cancelled by the aoristic time of the event. [...] through much of the Western tradition oil paint is treated primarily as an *erasive* medium. What it must first erase is the surface of the picture-plane [...]. The pigment must equally obey a second erasive imperative, and cover its own tracks: [...] stroke conceals canvas, as stroke conceals stroke. [...] whatever may have been the improvisational logic of the painting's construction, this existence of the image in its own time, of duration, of practice, of the body, is negated by never referring the marks on canvas to their place in the vanished sequence of local inspirations, but only to the twin axes of a temporality outside

> *durée*: on the one hand, the moment of origin, of the founding perception; and on the other, the moment of closure, of receptive passivity.[44]

This is contrasted with Chinese painting since the fifth century AD which, for Bryson, has been 'predicated on the acknowledgement and indeed the cultivation of deictic markers' such as the visibility of the 'constitutive strokes' of the brush, and the expression of 'the liquidity and immediate flow of the ink'.[45] This means that 'the work of production is constantly displayed in the wake of its traces', and in this formulation would 'apply only to a *performing art*' in the Western tradition.[46]

Bryson's book has come under heavy criticism since its publication, especially for its ambitious but at times sketchily substantiated attack on Gombrich's notions of correction and schema, and his lack of reference to Panofsky's different orders of iconological analysis.[47] His account of deixis has been accused of being too reductively analysed in the opposing traditions of Western and Chinese paintings; David Ebitz points out the arbitrary notations on Vermeer's paintings and Alex Potts raises Vasari's dialectic of viewing Titian's art as counter-examples to Bryson's argument of the absence of deictic time in the history of Western painting. But Bryson's notion of deixis remains very productive for considering the intersection of perception and depiction in an artwork and, as noted by Bal, gives the possibility of 'an interdisciplinary analysis of the visual domain as well as the literary, without the reductive detour via language'.[48] This is because all deictic terms as understood in linguistics must fall back on the deictic pronouns 'I' or 'you' which establish, first and foremost, the 'act of individual discourse in which it is pronounced', and by this designate the speaker as subject; as such, Émile Benveniste argues that 'I' and 'you' are 'distinguished from all other designations a language articulates in that *they do not refer to a concept or to an individual*'.[49] Extending from this thought, deixis provides an indexical framework in the visual arts to point to the relation between the viewing of the artwork and the process in which the deictic marker is created, rather than to a specific artist in a specific context of creation. This is a relation of reciprocity — that 'I becomes you in the address of the one who in his turn designates himself as I' — and, for Benveniste, constitutes the notion of personhood.[50]

Deixis thus provides a very promising framework within which to investigate how perception and depiction work together to make and un-make a figure in close relation to the position of viewing the artwork; it not only interrogates what constitutes figures and perspectives in artworks, but how these notions are closely associated with aspects of narrativity and subject-object relations. In this sense, deixis approaches the effects of Puchner's modernist theatrical diegesis in framing, controlling and interrupting the mimetic space. In fact, some visual theorists have explicitly considered the relation between deixis and diegesis in visual art, but with a reference to diegesis more generally as the world of the narrative or the content of representation in the artwork. For instance, Bal investigates in 'Second-person Narrative' whether a largely deictic painting, such as those of the abstract expressionists Pollock and de Kooning, can be seen in the light of a first-person narrative, as opposed to a third-person narrative in diegetic paintings that eliminate such 'emphatic inscription(s) of the hand of the artist'.[51] Ernst van Alphen further contrasts modes of looking at Bacon's triptych paintings in terms of diegetic narratives and 'apostrophic' or 'metonymic' narratives; the former refers to narratives based on perceiving 'the events acted out by the figures in the painting' and the latter refers to those that emerge from the 'diegetic narrative about perception' being 'doubled in relation to the viewer'.[52] Clearly, Alphen's 'apostrophic' narrative troubles any convenient categorization and delineation of the effects of 'deixis' and 'diegesis' on the depiction and perception of visual art; in this sense, it intersects with Puchner's framework of mimesis and diegesis, in which their effects on each other in modernist theatre cannot be clearly prised apart, as observed in *Happy Days*.

Positioning Residual Figuration

This book develops the notion of residual figuration in Beckett and Giacometti by drawing from diegesis and deixis as concepts through which perception and depiction can be compared across processes of creation and performance in different media. Chapter 1 begins by considering the role of scale and frame in creating distances and distancing in Beckett's television play *Eh Joe* and Giacometti's late busts of Annette and Eli Lotar. Chapter 2 concentrates on the use of lines and linear forms in a selection of lithographs from *Paris sans fin* and the dramaticules *Come and Go* and *Play*, and examines the ways in which such lines transfer and translate senses, spaces and narratives. Finally, Chapter 3 analyses the dynamics of figure and ground in creating types of hollow focalizations in the radio plays *All That Fall* and *Embers* and a selection of Giacometti's Diego paintings. In my conclusion, I propose residual figuration as a mode of inter-medial reading that develops rhetorical figures and pushes conceptions of eloquence and personhood.

My study has benefited greatly from existing comparative scholarship on Beckett and Giacometti. Of these, three broad strands of comparative reading have been particularly significant in shaping my eventual point of entry into this field: the existential and phenomenological, the aesthetic and philosophical, and the relational.

The first strand of reading takes the shared historical background of the two artists in Paris of the 1930s-60s as its point of entry. Within this context, existentialism and phenomenology emerge as two main ways of thinking about the two artists not just comparatively, but individually.[53] This mode of comparison can be seen most clearly in Matti Megged's pioneering study, *Dialogue in the Void*, which argues that what distinguished the two artists from their contemporaries were their shared obsessions, aspirations and certain unique traits in their works.[54] Chief among these are 'a fear of the void and a need for dialogue in or with the void', which Megged identifies through Beckett's use of a 'language in exile' and Giacometti's use of stage and dialogue in his sculptures.[55]

While my approach clearly differs in its point of entry from that of Megged, it benefits from his ways of discussing language and space across verbal and visual works. Taking up Beckett's 'Texts for Nothing' as an example, Megged shows that Beckett's use of language is 'independent of normal colloquium, loses even its grip on grammar, syntax, punctuation', and is 'exiled from the speaker himself'; even though these words fail to say anything, they are still spoken 'for their own sake' and 'the monologue becomes, rather, a dialogue in (or to) the void'.[56] This can be seen, Megged continues, in the use of the stage as an 'imaginary space' in Giacometti's surrealist works such as *Projet pour une place* [Model for a Square] (1932) and *On ne joue plus* [No More Play] (1932). On this stage, the 'totality of life' exists as an 'independent and self-sufficient reality' that 'bears no resemblance to the objective world'; Giacometti's figures can be seen as 'trying to establish a dialogue, albeit mute and probably doomed to failure' with the empty space or the void that surrounds them.[57] Therefore, the existential 'void' in Beckett and Giacometti is, for Megged, a space that surprisingly engages the figures in 'dialogue' both in speech and silence. My remaining chapters will develop this compelling interaction of space, dialogue and void through relations of subjectivity by way of deixis and diegesis.

The next strand of comparative reading is characterized by taking an aesthetic or philosophical context as its point of entry to comparative reading. This context need not be one that is historically shared; rather, it serves as a discursive framework to discuss certain similarities in the works of both men. Manfred Milz's study shows such an undertaking by using Bergson's vitalist philosophy as a framework to discussing the works that the artists produced between 1929 and 1936 (the surrealist works of Giacometti and the prose and aesthetic writings of Beckett).[58] It is through Bergson, Milz argues, that these works can be seen to engage in an aesthetic dialogue concerning the interior of surfaces even before the two men actually met. However, like Michael Sollars's study which proposes an aesthetic zone of the absurd in Beckett, Giacometti and Kafka derived through cognitive poetics, readings of this strand are hard-pressed to justify their taking a discursive framework as the starting point of comparison and, as a result, can appear rather ambitious.[59] Hence, in recognition of these difficulties and the scope of my book, my analyses of the works will begin with the reception of figures as perceived and depicted; the common observations garnered from this reception then necessitate a mode of reading that could explain, compare, conceptualize and develop ideas derived from the interaction of figures and their figurations.

In this respect, I find my approach most closely affiliated with readings of the third strand which explore relations between art forms and life-writing in close proximity to positions of reading, set within the larger framework of comparative criticism.[60] In particular, Timothy Mathews's writing appears to be the most illuminating in considering the position of the reader or the viewer in relation to the works, which in themselves incorporate different levels of focalization and frames of distancing.[61] These differences, Mathews argues, can be seen as translations of senses and experiences into style, which in turn generates a writing of history 'without the pretension to understand it'.[62] These uncertainties are aligned with the viewer's positions of approaching the works, which entail continuous attempts to understand and the necessary suspension of such attempts by the works themselves. For instance, he compares the reader's uncertainty in comprehending the relations between the eponymous Watt and Mr Knott in the permutations and frustrations presented in the piano-tuning episode, to the viewer's uncertainty in apprehending the proximity of Giacometti's sculptures in the face of their 'untouchable' materiality.[63] What Mathews articulates is a dimension of presence in these figures that derives from the reader's or the viewer's very act of approaching them; my book takes this as its starting point to further develop such dimensions through concepts that traverse works of different media and, in so traversing, provoke questions of narrativity and narration.

Notes to the Introduction

1. Samuel Beckett, *Waiting for Godot*, in *The Complete Dramatic Works* (London: Faber & Faber, 2006), pp. 7–88 (p. 61).
2. Cited in Akihiko Takeda, '"An Unknown Country": Isaku Yanaihara's Giacometti Diaries', in *Giacometti: Critical Essays*, ed. by Peter Read and Julie Kelly (London: Routledge, 2016), pp. 187–207 (p. 194).
3. Samuel Beckett, *The Unnamable* (New York: Grove, 1978), p. 179.
4. Their works appear in numerous issues of *Transition*, but no. 21 (1932) features both Beckett ('Sedendo et quiesciendo') and Giacometti (*Circuit* and *Suspended Ball*).
5. George Reavey and James Knowlson, 'George Reavey and Samuel Beckett's Early Writing: Edited Transcription of an Interview with George Reavey by James Knowlson, 6 August 1971', *Journal of Beckett Studies*, 2 (1977), 9–14 (p. 10). Hugo Daniel, 'Samuel Beckett, Alberto Giacometti (Work) in Progress', in *Giacometti Beckett: Rater encore. Rater mieux* (Lyon: Fage, 2020), pp. 9–34 (p. 24).
6. Samuel Beckett, letter to Georges Duthuit, Ussy, 10 September 1951, reproduced in Samuel Beckett, *Les Années Godot: lettres 1941–1956*, edited by George Craig and others (Paris: Gallimard, 2011), pp. 322–23; Jean Genet, *L'Atelier d'Alberto Giacometti* (Paris: L'Arbalète, 1963).
7. James Olney, 'Beckett's "Neither" & Giacometti's Figurine entre deux boîtes qui sont des maisons', *Daedalus*, 143 (2014), 77–84; Fred Miller Robinson, '"An Art of Superior Tramps": Beckett and Giacometti', *Centennial Review* (1981), 331–44; Peter Gidal, 'Beckett & Others & Art: A System', *Samuel Beckett Today/ Aujourd'hui*, 11 (2001), 303–14.
8. Matti Megged, *Dialogue in the Void: Beckett and Giacometti* (New York: Lumen Books, 1985); Andrea Pinotti, 'Soltanto l'essenziale: Beckett e Giacometti', *Quaderni di acme*, 97 (2007), 263–80.
9. Samuel Beckett, *Catastrophe*, in The *Complete Dramatic Works* (London: Faber & Faber, 2006), pp. 455–62 (p. 459).
10. Ibid. pp. 459–60.
11. Ibid. p. 460.
12. Jim Hansen, 'Samuel Beckett's Catastrophe and the Theater of Pure Means', *Contemporary Literature*, 49 (2008), 660–82 (p. 680).
13. For a discussion of how this looking implicates spectator identification, sympathy and resistance, see Anna McMullan, 'Performing Vision(s): Perspectives on Spectatorship in Beckett's Theatre', in *Samuel Beckett: A Casebook*, ed. by Jennifer M. Jeffers (London: Garland Publishing, 1998), pp. 133–58; Angela Moorjani, 'Directing or in-Directing Beckett: Or What Is Wrong with *Catastrophe*'s Director?', *Samuel Beckett Today/ Aujourd'hui*, 15 (2005), 187–99.
14. H. Porter Abbott, 'Tyranny and Theatricality: The Example of Samuel Beckett', *Theatre Journal*, 40 (1988), 77–87; Paul Sheehan, 'A World without Monsters: Beckett and the Ethics of Cruelty', in *Beckett and Ethics*, ed. by Russell Smith (London: Continuum, 2008), pp. 86–101.
15. I have elsewhere discussed how this can also be seen as a staging of the middle voice of the verb 'to narrate'. See Lin Li, '"To Narrate" — a Verb in the Middle Voice?: Narrativity and Performance in Samuel Beckett's Krapp's Last Tape and Ohio Impromptu', *Narrative*, 28 (2020), 289–303.

16. Samuel Beckett, *Ohio Impromptu*, in *The Complete Dramatic Works*, pp. 443–48 (p. 447).
17. Ibid., pp. 447, 448. For a detailed analysis, see Elizabeth Klaver, 'Samuel Beckett's "Ohio Impromptu", "Quad," and "What Where": How It Is in the Matrix of Text and Television', *Contemporary Literature*, 32 (1991), 366–82.
18. See Susan Bennett, *Theatre Audiences: A Theory of Production and Reception* (New York: Routledge, 2013).
19. For a detailed reading of this applause, see Craig N. Owens, 'Applause and Hiss: Implicating the Audience in Samuel Beckett's "Rockaby" and "Catastrophe"', *The Journal of the Midwest Modern Language Association*, 36 (2003), 74–81.
20. Steven Connor, *Beckett, Modernism and the Material Imagination* (Cambridge: Cambridge University Press, 2014), p. 9. For Sloterdijk's use, see Peter Sloterdijk, *Sphären III: Plurale Sphärologie: Schäume* (Frankfurt: Suhrkamp, 2004), pp. 74–88.
21. Connor, *Beckett, Modernism and the Material Imagination*, p. 9.
22. Christopher Bedford, 'Alberto Giacometti', in *The Fran and Ray Stark Collection of 20th-century Sculpture at the J. Paul Getty Museum*, ed. by Antonia Boström (Los Angeles: J. Paul Getty Museum, 2008), pp. 79–81 (p. 79).
23. David Sylvester, *Looking at Giacometti* (London: Pimlico, 1994), p. 228.
24. While most sources, including Giacometti himself, refer to seven figures being cast, the Alberto and Annette Giacometti Foundation states only six, omitting *Standing Woman III*. See Alberto and Annette Giacometti Foundation <http://www.fondation-giacometti.fr/files/ea66a51a2c18130488d6b97267bddd98250a71e5.pdf> [accessed 4 May 2016].
25. The only exception that has been noted by scholars is *Figurine entre deux boîtes qui sont des maisons* (1950). This work frames a walking woman figure within an overt material structure, and is characteristic of other works made during the same time such as *Quatre figurines sur base* and *La Femme au chariot*.
26. Alex Potts, *The Sculptural Imagination: Figurative, Modernist, Minimalist* (New Haven, CT: Yale University Press, 2000), p. 122. See also Florence Quideau, 'Origins of Modernism in French Romantic Sculpture: David D'Angers, Dantan-Jeune, Daumier and Préault' (unpublished PhD Dissertation, Rutgers University, 2011); David J. Getsy, *Body Doubles: Sculpture in Britain, 1877–1905* (New Haven, CT: Yale University Press, 2004). On the tactility-opticality debate, see for example David J. Getsy, 'Tactility or Opticality, Henry Moore or David Smith: Herbert Read and Clement Greenberg on the Art of Sculpture, 1956', *Sculpture Journal*, 17 (2008), 75–88; Herbert Read, *The Art of Sculpture* (New York: Pantheon books, 1956); Clement Greenberg, *The Collected Essays and Criticism, Volume 3: Affirmations and Refusals, 1950–1956* (Chicago, IL: University of Chicago Press, 1995).
27. Martin Puchner, *Stage Fright: Modernism, Anti-theatricality, and Drama* (Baltimore, MD: Johns Hopkins University Press, 2002), pp. 24–26; Jon Erickson, 'The Ghost of the Literary in Recent Theories of Text and Performance', *Theatre Survey*, 47 (2006), 245–51 (p. 245).
28. See Norman Bryson, *Vision and Painting: The Logic of the Gaze* (New Haven, CT: Yale University Press, 1983), pp. 88–92; *The Practice of Cultural Analysis: Exposing Interdisciplinary Interpretation*, ed. by Mieke Bal, with Bryan Gonzales (Stanford, CA: Stanford University Press, 1999), pp. 11–12; David Carrier, *The Aesthete in the City: The Philosophy and Practice of American Abstract Painting in the 1980s* (University Park: Pennsylvania State University Press, 1994), p. 220.
29. Mieke Bal, *Reading 'Rembrandt': Beyond the Word-image Opposition* (Amsterdam: Amsterdam University Press, 2006). Her development of deixis can be found in numerous later works such as: *Quoting Caravaggio: Contemporary Art, Preposterous History* (Chicago: University of Chicago Press, 1999); *Endless Andness: The Politics of Abstraction According to Ann Veronica Janssens* (London: Bloomsbury, 2013).
30. Puchner, *Stage Fright*, p. 22.
31. Ibid.
32. Ibid. p. 24.
33. Ibid.
34. Ibid. p. 25.
35. Ibid. pp. 26, 160.

36. Ibid. p. 26.
37. Ibid.
38. Ibid. p. 163.
39. James Knowlson, *'Happy Days': The Production Notebook of Samuel Beckett* (London: Faber & Faber, 1985), p. 16.
40. Emile Benveniste, 'Subjectivity in Language', in *Problems in General Linguistics*, trans. by Mary Elizabeth Meek (Coral Gables, FL: University of Miami Press, 1971), pp. 223–30 (p. 226).
41. Bal, *Endless Andness*, p. 58.
42. Bryson, *Vision and Painting,* pp. 89–92.
43. Bal, *Reading 'Rembrandt'*, pp. 32–33. See Charles S. Peirce, 'Logic as Semiotic: The Theory of Signs', in *Semiotics: An Introductory Anthology*, ed. by R. E. Innis (Bloomington: Indiana University Press, 1985), pp. 1–23.
44. Bryson, *Vision and Painting,* pp. 89–93.
45. Ibid. p. 89.
46. Ibid. p. 92.
47. See especially David Ebitz, 'Review: Vision and Painting: The Logic of the Gaze by Norman Bryson', *The Art Bulletin*, 69 (1987), 155–58; Alex Potts, 'Difficult Meanings', *The Burlington Magazine*, 129 (1987), 29–32; P. N. Humble, 'Review of Vision and Painting: The Logic of the Gaze by Norman Bryson', *The Journal of Aesthetics and Art Criticism*, 43 (1984), 219–21.
48. Mieke Bal, 'Introduction', in *The Practice of Cultural Analysis*, ed. by Bal and Gonzales, pp.1–14 (p. 12).
49. Émile Benveniste, 'Subjectivity in Language', in *Problems in General Linguistics*, pp. 223–30 (p. 226). Emphasis in original.
50. Ibid. p. 224.
51. Mieke Bal, 'Second-person Narrative', *Paragraph*, 19 (1996), 179–204 (p. 180).
52. Ernst Van Alphen, 'The Narrative of Perception and the Perception of Narrative', *Poetics Today*, 11 (1990), 483–509 (p. 508).
53. For both Beckett and Giacometti, see also Daniel, 'Samuel Beckett, Alberto Giacometti (Work) in Progress'; Robinson, '"An Art of Superior Tramps"'; Pinotti, 'Soltanto l'essenziale'. For Giacometti, see Julia Kelly, 'Alberto Giacometti, Michel Leiris and the Myths of Existentialism', in *Giacometti Critical Essays,* ed. by Peter Read and Julia Kelly (Ashgate: Farnham, 2009), pp. 151–70; Jean-Paul Sartre, *Essays in Aesthetics*, ed. and trans. by Wade Baskin (New York: Open Road Media, 2012); Michael Scriven, 'Ideological Art Criticism: Sartre and Giacometti', in *Jean-Paul Sartre: Politics and Culture in Postwar France,* (Basingstoke: Macmillan, 2016), pp. 113–32. For Beckett, see Steven Connor, 'Beckett and Sartre: The Nauseous Character of All Flesh', in *Beckett, Modernism and the Material Imagination,* (Cambridge: Cambridge University Press, 2014), pp. 27–47; Matthew Feldman, 'Beckett, Sartre and Phenomenology', *Limit(e) Beckett* (2010), 1–26; Edith Kern, *Existential Thought and Fictional Technique: Kierkegaard, Sartre, Beckett* (New Haven, CT: Yale University Press, 1970).
54. Megged, *Dialogue in the Void,* p. 1.
55. Ibid.
56. Ibid. p. 16.
57. Ibid., p. 21.
58. Manfred Milz, *Samuel Beckett und Alberto Giacometti: das Innere Als Oberfläche. Ein ästhetischer Dialog im Zeichen Schöpferischer Entzweiungsprozesse (1929–1936)* (Würzburg: Königshausen & Neumann, 2006). This study remains untranslated. For a review in English, see Thomas Hunkeler, 'Review of Recent Beckett Criticism in Germany', *Journal of Beckett Studies*, 19 (2010), 273–76.
59. Michael David Sollars, 'Kafkaesque Absurdity in the Aesthetics of Beckett and Giacometti', *Enthymema* (2013), 71–82.
60. Here I take the lead from works such as *Provocation and Negotiation: Essays in Contemporary Criticism*, ed. by Gesche Ipsen, Timothy Mathews, and Dragana Obradovic (Amsterdam: Rodopi, 2013). For such comparative criticism dealing specifically with Beckett and Giacometti, see also Olney, 'Beckett's "Neither" & Giacometti's "Figurine entre deux boîtes qui sont des maisons"'.

61. Timothy Mathews, 'Walking with Angels in Giacometti and Beckett', *L'Esprit Créateur*, 47 (2007), 29–42. See also Timothy Mathews, *Alberto Giacometti: The Art of Relation* (London: I. B.Tauris, 2014).
62. Mathews, 'Walking with Angels in Giacometti and Beckett'', p. 38.
63. Ibid. p. 31.

CHAPTER 1

Scale and Frame in *Eh Joe* and the Late Busts

> 'When we say vos, or "you",' says Nigidius, 'we make a movement of the mouth suitable to the meaning of the word; for we gradually protrude the tips of our lips and direct the impulse of the breath towards those with whom we are speaking. But on the other hand, when we say nos, or "us", we do not pronounce the word with a powerful forward impulse of the voice, nor with the lips protruded, but we restrain our breath and our lips, so to speak, within ourselves. The same thing happens in the words tu or "thou", ego or "I", tibi "to thee", and mihi "to me". For just as when we assent or dissent, a movement of the head or eyes corresponds with the nature of the expression, so too in the pronunciation of these words there is a kind of natural gesture made with the mouth and breath.'
>
> — Aulus Gellius, *Attic Nights*, Book 10[1]

The 1977 BBC2 broadcast *Shades* was composed of two of Beckett's television plays *Ghost Trio* and *...but the clouds...*, and a television adaptation of *Not I* by Billie Whitelaw.[2] While introducing the programme, Melvyn Bragg compared the 'strong visual images' in Beckett's television plays to the works of Giacometti, specifically to one of his *Women of Venice* sculptures. According to Bragg, the comparison illustrated the way in which the intention of neither artist was to 'make images that are like life'; rather, they aimed to 'concentrate' and 'minimize' the images to present a reality that is constantly 'failing', 'disintegrating' and slipping through our fingers. However, such a comparison raises questions: how can the processes of concentration and minimization in the televisual and sculptural media be compared, and how do they give the impression of a disintegrating whole in their resulting creations?

Bragg did not expand on his points, and existing comparative scholarship on Beckett's television plays, while extensive, has largely compared them to paintings.[3] Some clues, however, can be gleaned from these writings as to the subtractive composition of the images, many of which refer to Deleuze's 'The Exhausted', first published in 1992 as a coda to the French translation of *Quad*.[4] In this essay, Deleuze argues for the distillation of a 'language III' in Beckett's work that is composed of the 'form' and 'process' of the image or space, rather than the 'sublimeness of its content'.[5] This language of images and spaces is found par excellence in the television plays, and it has the capacity to loosen 'the grip of words' in Beckett's 'language I' (found in the novels) and dry up 'the oozing of voices' of 'language II' (novels, theatre and radio) so as to 'disengage itself from memory and reason'.[6] This process of disengaging, writes Deleuze, involves both synthesis and dissipation; the image-space gathers up and exhausts the possibilities with language and voices by making them become 'image, movement, song, poem'.[7]

The impetus of that making-becoming is also the process by which the image-space takes shape. *Quad*, for instance, eventually exhausts space not through repetition per se, but by extenuating the possibility of encounter within it. This is done by way of the tension created between the figures never meeting and the repetition that gradually takes on the shape of musical refrain, canon or ensemble.[8] Here, movement creates a space-image that in its making-becoming, simultaneously propels yet dissipates the non-encounter; the fusing of perception and form through movement creates an exhausted image that is torn from language, but which remains a 'process' rather than an 'object'.[9] Lydia Rainford points out that what is particularly useful and intriguing about Deleuze's reading is this emphasis on the final realization of the image as one poised on 'a complete rupturing of identity and memory' rather than a 'breakthrough into concrete representation of experience'.[10] This, Bryden argues, shows Deleuze's awareness of his having to respond to words in the televisual medium with 'an alternate level of responsiveness', as shown through his 'tripartite division of language'.[11]

Deleuze's reading of Beckett's television plays shows that the subtractive composition of the image necessarily implicates the interaction of perceived and depicted space and time, and it is this observation that forms my point of entry into a comparison between how figures are created and perceived in Beckett's *Eh Joe* and Giacometti's late bronze busts. In both cases, this operates in relation to presenting distances and movements of distancing. While it seems at first glance that both media involve the space and time of the viewer in markedly contrasting ways — a viewer remains passively seated in front of a television screen while she or he must walk around a sculpture in an exhibition room — further investigation will reveal that these differences are not as straightforward. In fact, of the three media that Beckett and Giacometti each used in creating dramatic texts and visual art, it was only in the televisual and the sculptural that scale and frame played such a central role in creating figures. In particular, both artists used scale and frame to explore how different perceptions and depictions of distance and distancing can be created between the space of the viewer and the space of the figures. It is the manipulation of these spatial impressions that makes the televisual and sculptural images appear 'concentrated', 'minimized' and yet at times in the process of 'disintegrating'.

Scale and Frame in Beckett's Television Plays

For a start, the televisual medium seems to have encouraged Beckett to explore the effects of presenting figures, faces or parts of faces at an extremely close distance otherwise unattainable in a theatrical space. For instance, Whitelaw's mouth fills the entire frame of the television in the screen production of *Not I*, which is in contrast to the minute mouth that appears to be dangling mid-air when the play is viewed in the theatre. Whitelaw's mouth saturates the screen in magnified proportions due to the extreme close-up shot, and appears unreal and distorted at moments when the mouth shuts or lips clasp. The unrelenting characteristic of Mouth is magnified by the compression of distance in the viewer's act of looking; our eyes have no room to rest or wander within the confines of the frame as they are constantly confronted by a mouth that appears to be right in front of them.[12]

Unlike the mouth that is staged, this magnified mouth on screen produces a voice that appears to be acousmatic rather than disembodied. An acousmatic voice is a voice whose source and origin one cannot see or identify, and as Mladen Dolar puts it, is a voice 'in search of an origin' or a 'body'.[13] These differing impressions come about as a result of the different expectations we have of the image due to Mouth's contrasting spaces of projection: the theatre-goer expects and imagines the minute, lingering mouth in the distance to belong to the body of a performer sharing the same theatre space, but the mouth that the television viewer is faced with is a close-up effect that, in its prolonged stasis, suggests pictorial surface rather than an actual human body from which the close-up is derived.[14] It disorientates any sense of spatial or figural grounding and thus loses its human form; a comparison can here be drawn to the surrealist lips of Dali (for instance, in *Mae West's Face Which May be Used as a Surrealist Apartment*) and Man Ray (*Observatory Time — The Lovers*), which in travelling and creating connections across imaginary spaces, become new entities that lose their facial origins.[15] Thus, while the theatrical Mouth negates any fixed sense of subjectivity, an observation further encouraged by the helpless gesturing of the Auditor as an 'other to the Mouth',[16] the televisual Mouth omits the counterpoint figure of Auditor altogether, and displaces this dialectic disembodiment with an acousmatic obliteration of voice from origin via pictorial flattening.[17]

Yet, at the same time, Mouth on television is also framed as a kind of object or target of our looking by the rectangular frame of the television screen and the depth of the television set. In fact, similarly to how the vanishing point of Dali's *Mae West* painting leads into the face, the depth and frame of the television box of *Not I* invite the viewer not merely to look at the mouth, but to look into or inside it. Through this process, Mouth creates another frame within the frame of the television set, thus situating and inflecting three-dimensional space by way of two-dimensional boundaries. By making the mouth appear to be frame, surface and object, the close-up, thus, plays with relations of distancing between the space of the viewer's viewing, and the space in which the mouth is situated.

It is essential in any analysis of Beckett's television plays to bear in mind also the sort of television screens on which these plays were being watched in the 1970s.[18] The common household television set then was a bulky wooden-framed box frequently installed as part of a cabinet or on its own with an independent stand. It had a slightly convex screen that usually had rounded edges and protruded from its frame; this usually resulted in an interrupted visibility of television images due to the refraction of exterior light that cast reflections on the screen.

There are two aspects involved in the watching of these particular television sets that are integral to the perception of scale and frame in the television images. First, the prominent, rectangular frame of the television enhanced the pictorial quality of any screen image by demarcating its boundaries and embedding it within the television set or frame. Most of these sets were rather bulky and some from the 1950s to 60s had doors that closed over the television screen which gave the television set, which was called colloquially 'the box', an added dimension of staging as compared to a modern-day flat plasma screen with a sleek, minimal frame. In fact, Beckett had pointedly referred to the television as a box which he had thought more suited to capturing individual faces and actions than characters set within a larger space. In response to McWhinnie's BBC television production of *Waiting for Godot* in 1961, Beckett had said:

> My play [...] wasn't written for this box. My play was written for small men locked in a big space. Here you're all too big for the place. [...] You see, you could write a very good play for television about a woman knitting. You'd go from the face to the knitting, from the knitting to the face.[19]

For Beckett, the character in televisual space is a subject engaged in domestic interior space — here reflecting the viewer's own space of viewing and the activities that s/he might be engaged in while viewing — rather than an object that inhabits a fraction of a larger exterior space. The use of the moving camera as a depiction of and an interception between figure and action is explored most clearly in *Eh Joe* and *Ghost Trio*, but vanishes in the remaining plays *...but the clouds...*, *Quad* and *Nacht und Träume,* where the camera does not, or hardly, moves.

The second factor was the distance from which people watched these television sets. Because the picture quality was usually grainy and the use of the household remote control was not yet widespread, families might gather very near the television set for ease of watching the programme and adjusting the volume and channel knobs at the same time. The televisual image would, therefore, have been perceived in a different way on those television sets as compared to modern-day television sets due to these factors of scale and framing. In the case of *Not I*, the acousmatic impact of the static, surreal image would, no doubt, have been strongly enhanced due to the close distance from which the mouth confronted the viewer relentlessly from inside a screen-box, and within the closed setting of a sitting room. In addition, transmission interferences and unsynchronized audio-visual images were very real concerns during this time; these demanded not only a shorter distance of viewing but also a greater degree of concentration, thus intensifying the experience of 'television' as 'vision from a distance' in comparison to present-day digital televisions. In this sense, television-watching in the 1960s and 70s involved specific constraints of staging and framing that inherently engineered a larger degree of concentration and spectatorship. It became an act of looking in rather than one of merely watching; depth was generated by the position and constraints of reading the image.

Moving away from this brief social history of television and back to scale and frame, the second way in which Beckett employed them was to contrast and alternate between rapid shifts in camera perspectives. In *Ghost Trio*, for instance, the viewer is

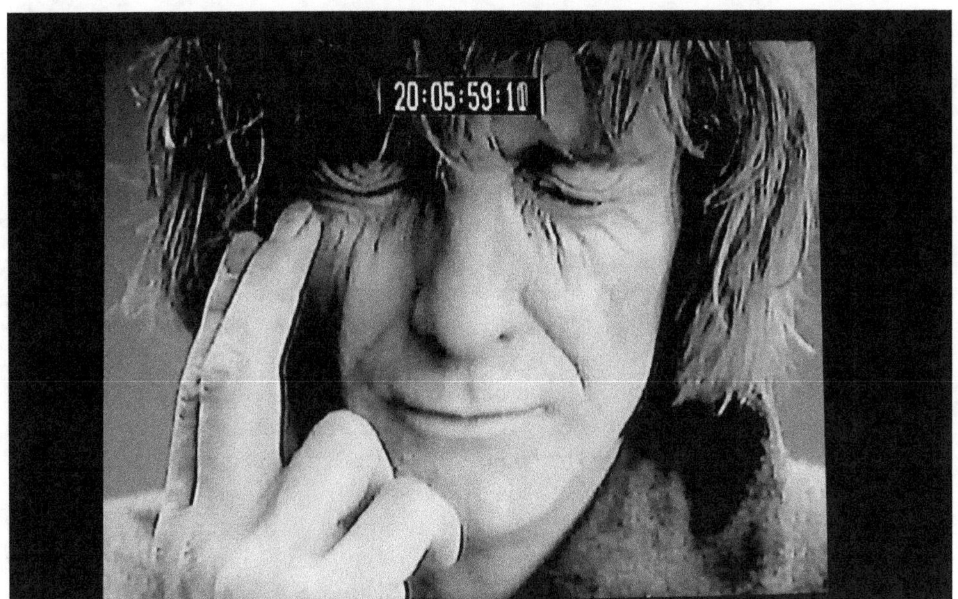

Fig. 1.1. Still from *Ghost Trio*, in *Shades* (BBC, 1977), performed by Ronald Pickup.

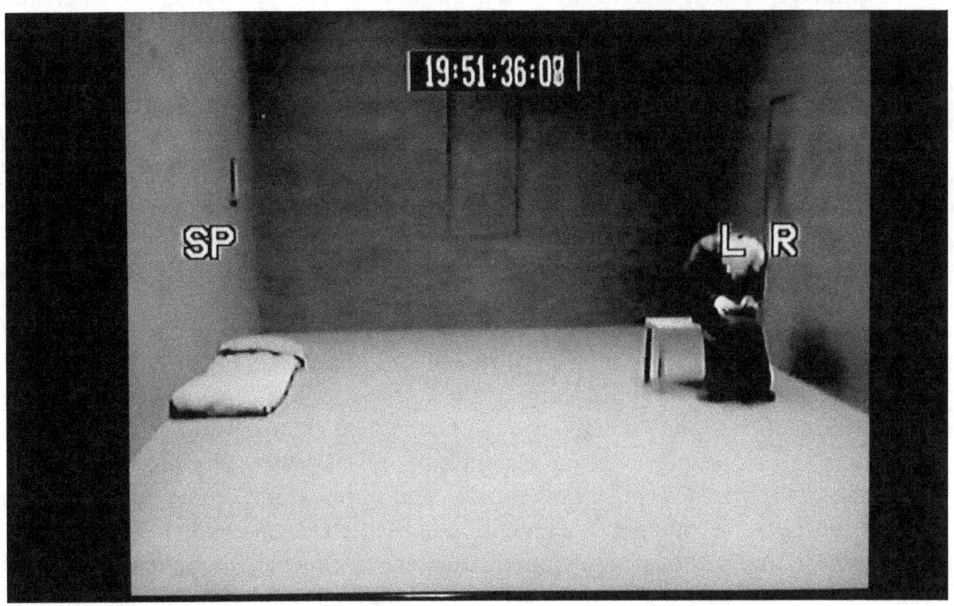

Fig. 1.2. Establishing shot of *Ghost Trio* (BBC, 1977).

confronted with a sudden cut to a close-up shot of F's face in the mirror (see figure 1.1) in the third part of the play, 'Re-action', after having only been able to see his head and body from a distance up to that point of the play (see figure 1.2). With this close-up shot, the viewer makes a sudden swerve in the focalization of F as directed by the mobile camera: instead of following and looking at F from a distance, the viewer is now abruptly brought to face him up-close in his mirrored reflection. However, instead of inviting any form of identification with F — as would have been the case in the cinematic techniques of classical Hollywood cinema — the framing of the shot tightly circumscribes and limits the shot, emphasizing the flat, pictorial quality of F as image.[20] This is further heightened by the rupture in the positioning of the camera within the diegetic space: in showing F's inverted image, the camera lens supplants the position of the mirror itself and undercuts the spatial representation of the room. Due to this play in scale and framing by way of camera movement, F becomes a figure that cannot completely be grasped in space or seen as image.

Such figures and faces that are perceived as consciously distanced or flattened by way of camera perspectives also suffuse the other television plays, such as *...but the clouds...* and *Eh Joe*. In fact, the effect of spatial-undercutting created by camera perspectives in these plays is further intensified by the sparse and confined interiors of the filmed spaces, as seen in the boxed-up room of F. Like Mouth, which creates an organic frame in the middle of the television screen, these boxy rooms also mimic and emphasize the frame of the 1960s-70s television set, which makes it even harder to spatially place these largely static figures in relation to our position of viewing.

The third way in which Beckett manipulated scale and frame was in transposing long, still takes to create what might be called a perpetual deadening of the figures. This is a state of sustained stillness towards no perceivable end, and it is a recurrent motif in much of Beckett's prose and drama, perhaps most overtly in *Stirrings Still*. Due to its capacity to synthesize, separate and manipulate the visual and the aural with great immediacy and sustained duration, the television becomes the ideal vehicle to present this state of perpetual deadening.

The most striking way in which Beckett presented this was by using a combination of the long take and a static frame, and then repeating it with slight variations, as can be observed most acutely in *Quad* (where the second part is a repetition of the first except in slow motion and in black and white) and *Nacht und Träume* (where the second part is a repetition of the first in close-up). In this way, the state of deadening is stretched out and intensified, an effect analogous to the musical techniques of augmentation and transposition: augmentation is the re-presentation of a musical motif with proportionately longer values than in its first presentation, and transposition is the re-presentation of a motif in a different key or pitch. In re-presenting the original themes with a different colour, tone or mood, such techniques achieve a narrative effect of wandering and return, permutation and origin, without the introduction of new melodic material.[22] The televisual medium comes close to enacting visually these musical permutations not only due to its capacity to manipulate the visual and the aural with great immediacy and sustained duration, but also because it has the benefit of post-production editing. This can be seen in *Quad*, where it was the accident of post-production editing that actually gave rise to *Quad II* as the augmented, transposed form of *Quad I*. According to most accounts, after watching *Quad I* played back on a black and white monitor in slow motion during post-production, Beckett decided that this was *Quad I* a 'hundred thousand years later' and went on to create *Quad II*.[23] In a rare recorded conversation with Barney Rosset and John Reilly, Beckett even joked that if there were a *Quad III*, the figures would all be 'lying down', further supporting the observation of such perpetual deadening of figures as a kind of visual transposition that creates style through static and repetitive mimetic action.[24]

In fact, this state of perpetual deadening created by the long, still takes is further heightened by visual characteristics of the figures in the frame. In the case of the television adaptation of *What Where*, it was actually sculpture that was the point of departure for the figures. In a conversation about the Stuttgart production of *What Where* with his cameraman Jim Lewis, Beckett mentioned that V, which was originally intended to be a small megaphone onstage, should be replaced by an enlarged death mask resembling John Donne's statue in St Paul's Cathedral (see figure 1.3).[25] This sculpture was created after John Donne's death and is based on a drawing of him in his last days. According to Izaak Walton, Donne had posed for the drawing by standing on a pedestal fashioned as a funerary urn with the likeness of a dead body placed in a coffin.[26] Beckett had originally intended for all four figures (Bim, Bam, Bem and Bom) also to resemble the statue and move rigidly in the style of a 'mechanical ballet', but decided by May 1985 that there were not to be any figures left. In his words, it was 'everything down to the bare minimum [...] everything out but the faces'.[27] These enlarged, floating death masks nudge the figures towards an image almost-still, almost-dead and almost-absent, or, in Clov's words, the 'nearly finished'.[28] In this sense, the visual qualities of the figures can be seen to intensify the state of perpetual deadening created by the long, still take of the play.

There are, then, three main ways in which Beckett manipulated scale and frame in the television plays to generate spatial perceptions of distance and distancing between the viewer and the figure: the first in using the close-up, the second in contrasting and alternating between rapid shifts in camera perspectives, and the third in transposing long, still takes to create a state of sustained stillness, or what I call the perpetual deadening of figures. Giacometti likewise used scale and frame to shape spatial perceptions and depictions of his figures, making them appear 'concentrated', 'minimized', and yet in the process of 'disintegrating'. However, in order to compare such processes between the televisual and the sculptural, one must begin by making a distinction between the space of the viewer and the space of the figure in the two media.

As we have seen in our brief overview of Beckett's television plays, the space occupied by the viewer refers to the space in which the television play is watched, which in the context of the 1960s to 70s was usually the sitting room with the

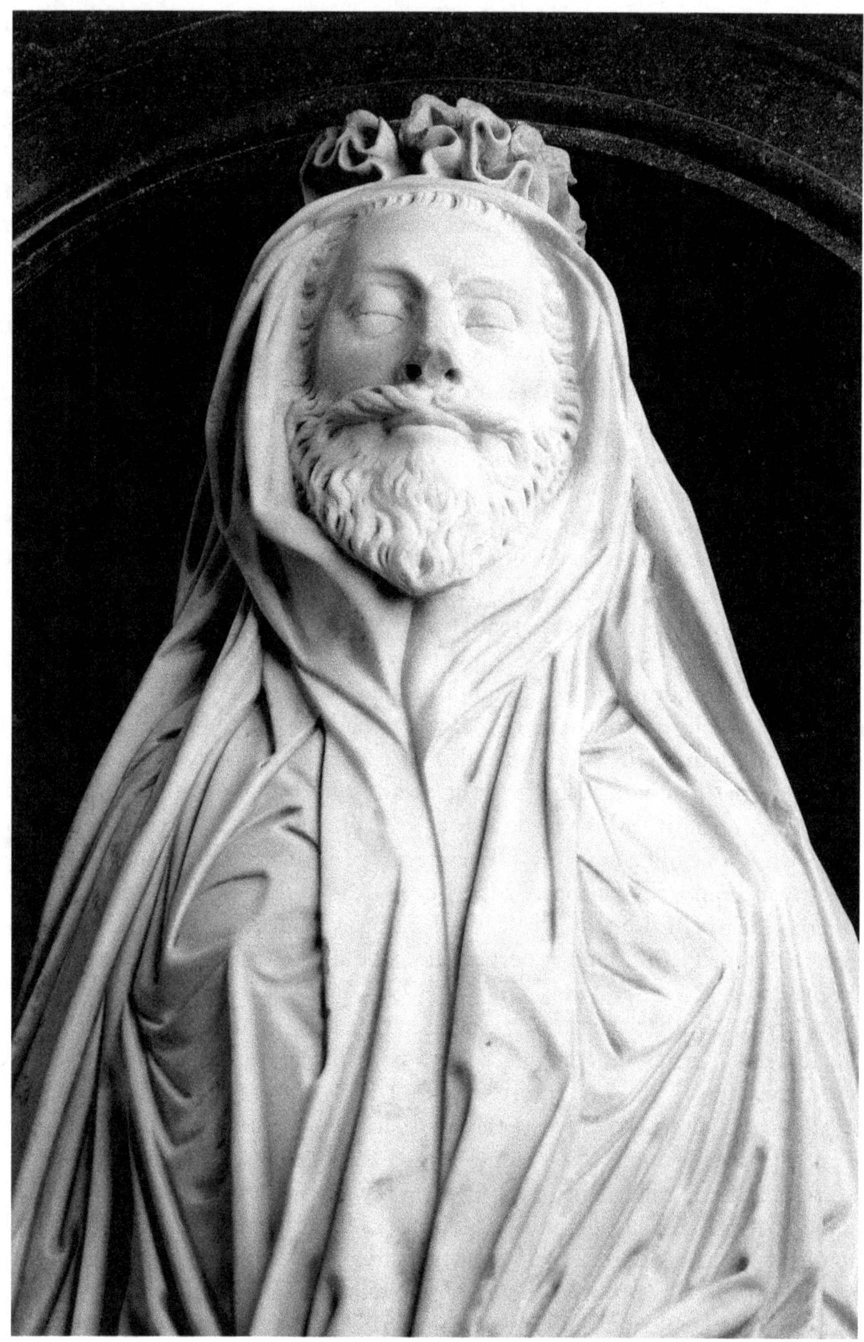

Fig. 1.3. Nicholas Stone, *Monument to the Poet John Donne*, 1632, marble, St Paul's Cathedral, London. © The Chapter of St Paul's Cathedral.

television set. The space of the figure in the play refers to the diegetic space of the figure: in *Ghost Trio* for instance, it is the sparse boxed-up room as seen in figure 1.2. However, in sculpture, the space of the figure and the space of the viewer is a shared physical space: this is the space in which the sculpture is placed, which could be a gallery in a museum or the courtyard of an exhibition venue. This shared physical space is both an actual, realistic space (a museum gallery for instance) or an implied diegetic space in which the figure is perceived to be situated due to a combination of artistic elements such as scale, size and base. This overlapping of spaces happens because the negative space for a sculpture is the actual three-dimensional space shared with the viewer; this is unlike the case for paintings and drawings where implied diegetic space is a result of the figure being in a negative space framed by the canvas or the print. Because of this, scale and frame become especially effective in creating and erasing perceptions of distance and distancing between the implied space that the sculpture occupies and the realistic space from which we apprehend it.

In the light of this, a sculpted figure can, therefore, be seen to be framed by two kinds of ground. The first is the background of the actual space against which the viewer sees it: at present usually a light-coloured wall of a museum, but it can change as the viewer moves or the sculpture is resituated. The second is the ground on which it stands, and which usually plays a significant role in creating its implied space: this is its base, which is usually permanent, but may also be provisional and contingent on exhibition and location formatting, as with a plinth.

Using scale and frame, Giacometti strove to integrate an unchanging sense of implied space surrounding the figure that would keep it precisely distanced regardless of how the spectator moved around it. He wanted to achieve in sculpture what came so naturally to painting: that a painted figure remained at the same implied distance from the viewer regardless of the various permutations of angles and distances from which it could be viewed. This impression of a fixedly distanced figure is what Sartre terms in his first essay on Giacometti, 'La Recherche de l'absolu' [The Quest for the Absolute] (1948), a 'situated appearance' which gives 'perceptible expression to pure presence'.[29] In his first essay on Giacometti, 'The Quest for the Absolute' (1948), Sartre asserts that the absolute in sculpture consisted of a human figure that could be apprehended all at once in a universal yet foreign way, such that it is '*already seen* but not as already seen by himself alone [...] just as a foreign language that we are trying to learn is already spoken'.[30] Giacometti, he claims, achieves this by creating a form of absolute distance by way of scale and elongation. In his works, distance, far from being an 'accident', 'isolation' or 'withdrawal', is a 'negation in the form of a *vacuum*'; this vacuum occurs '*from a plenum*' in sculpture, and comes close to achieving the notion of a '*true* void' in painting, in which figures are framed 'as a transparency' and are 'not solidly stitched but merely basted'.[31] These terms are not vague, Sartre asserts, for Giacometti gives us the precision of being, what he terms 'pure presence', precisely by methodically and repeatedly expounding the imprecision of perception in his works.

One of the ways in which Giacometti worked towards sculpting this absolute distance was by varying the proportion of the figure to its base, as he had once expressed in an interview in 1963:

> The sculpture I wanted to make of that woman was the very precise vision I'd had of her at the moment when I'd caught a glimpse of her in the street, from quite a distance. So I tended to make her the size she looked when she was at that distance. This took place in the Boulevard Saint-Michel, at midnight. I could see the enormous expanse of darkness above her, and some houses, so to reproduce the impression I'd had [...] I ought to have made an enormous base so that the ensemble would correspond to the vision.[32]

The proportion of the figure to the base becomes, for Giacometti, one way in which scale and frame are used to create the perception of distance in a sculpture. But more than that, for it is the perception of remaining at a distance that formed this 'vision'; the figure must be small because it is 'at that distance', but this smallness serves to interact with the base to 'correspond' to the 'vision'. But if by vision Giacometti refers to visual memory, then what this interaction strives to correspond to is already itself receding and in the distance; the 'very precise' perception of remaining at a distance that scale and frame serve to depict is, therefore, either unreliable or unfounded. This tendency towards self-effacement could begin to explain Giacometti's constant struggle to copy the 'residue of a vision' that hovers between 'disappearing' and 'coming into view', and which is, therefore, constantly 'remaking' itself.[33]

This struggle is seen most clearly through the different manipulations of scale and frame to create different styles of sculptures, starting from the minute figures of the war years. Assessing how notions of size, vision and distance were manipulated in such different ways over more than two decades will give a better understanding of how Giacometti arrived at a peculiar use of scale and frame to create acts of looking in his last busts of Annette and Eli Lotar.

Scale and Frame in Giacometti's Sculptures

From 1939 to 1945, Giacometti created tiny figurines which were so small (often to the height of just one centimetre) that they were at risk of crumbling at a single touch. These figures were usually placed on large pedestals and double bases that appeared to be completely disproportionate to the miniscule sizes of the figures. In fact, this disproportion shows depiction as a process of practice rather than an act of execution because it results from an obsessive subtraction of only the figure and not the base. According to David Sylvester who quotes Diego, Giacometti's younger brother, Giacometti would start 'on a plaster figure ten or twelve inches high and would end up again and again with a figure not more than about an inch high standing on a base whose size would have been normal for a figure he started with'.[34] These figures show Giacometti's attempts to materialize a vision of distance brought to its extreme; size was sacrificed to realize the thresholds of scale.

In 1945, Giacometti reportedly experienced a breakthrough in his artistic vision following a night at the cinema. According to him, this had happened at the news theatre in Montparnasse:

> First of all, I no longer knew what I was seeing on the screen: instead of its being figures, it was becoming black and white blobs, that's to say they were losing all meaning, and instead of looking at the screen I kept looking at my neighbours, who were becoming something altogether unknown. It was the reality around me that was the unknown, not what was happening on the screen. Going out on to the boulevard I had the feeling of being faced with something I had never seen before, with a complete change in reality — the unseen, the altogether unknown, the marvellous. The Boulevard Montparnasse took on the beauty of The Arabian Nights, fantastic, altogether unknown. And at the same time, the silence, an unbelievable sort of silence.[35]

Because of this experience, he began reconciling the 'phenomenological' dimensions of his minute sculptures with more 'normal' proportions of sculptures.[36] However, what is meant by 'normal' is the recognition of certain styles of figure representation rather than a realistic representation of the human body from life. According to Reinhold Hohl, Giacometti was, at this point, actively searching for a more 'finished' sculptural style due to the growing interest in public memorials after the war, and began to interrogate the artificial and hieratic characteristics of Egyptian and Etruscan sculpture.[37] This interrogation resulted in modifications not only to precise features of sculpted posture and appearance, but also to the frame of the human body itself; some of these included eschewing contrapposto, concentrating on a strong frontality of the heads, and attenuating the frame of the figure. However, Sylvester argues that the last feature is likely to be a stylistic debt to Cycladic sculpture, which frequently presents lateral attenuation that is 'more marked than the frontal'.[38] This creates an interesting counterpoint to understanding sculptural scale as a relation of the figure to its grounds, because such attenuation effectively renders the figure as an impression of a line or a plane from the profile view. The figure, thus, extends as part of its ground and also dissolves into it; this positions the figure as itself a continuation from or an operation of framing, which partially erases the comparative dimension of scale.

This overall shift in scale and style enhanced the pictorial quality of his sculptures, but also enforced a sense of authority by drawing the viewer's line of sight with the sculpted gaze. Such an effect is very clearly seen in some of his group portraits from 1947–50, such as *The Forest* (1950), where attenuated figures of different scales seem to rise up and exist in their own independent space from the same base. These figures look out frontally as if through a shared pictorial screen that melds into the exhibition space of the viewer. The juxtaposition of bust and figures of contrasting scales further gives the impression of cinematic long shots superimposed on close-ups. While the frontality of the figures arrests the directionality of the viewer's act of looking in actual space, the individual figures appear to eliminate and shed superfluous filling to the extent that the sculpture's residual frame of crevasses and knobs seem to erode into the implied negative space around it. This conflation of negative and actual space by way of juxtaposing contrasting scales and frontality creates perceptions of distancing within a single work.

This gradual shift in scale and style from the late 1940s to the mid-1950s also resulted in the insertion of duration into repeated figures belonging to the same series. As implied by the long take of the *Woman of Venice* sculpture from the base to the head in the BBC production *Shades*, the perception of sculpture is, first and foremost, temporally bound into and across the space in which it is exhibited. But there is a second aspect to sculptural duration that is essential to understanding Giacometti's works, and that is the unceasing re-working of the same model, from the same distance and, sometimes, even from the same mass of clay over a long stretch of time.

The *Women of Venice* sculptures make a good case in point. As a result of their increasingly being staged and exhibited as individual sculptures, it becomes easy to forget that *Women of Venice* was in fact conceived of and exhibited by Giacometti as a 'work in progress' of ten standing female sculptures, split into two groups of four and six, for part of his installation at the Venice Biennale in 1956. Each sculpture is an incarnation of the other for they were all moulded under the same conditions using the same material:

> Specifically for the *Biennale* in Venice Giacometti prepared a standing figure of a woman, over a metre in height, that he modelled in many versions. On each occasion he used the same armature and mass of clay (every morning Diego took a plaster cast of the previous night's work) but the figures were always different in expression and height (from 1.05 to 1.56 metres). In all, there were more than fifteen states of this *Woman of Venice* (*Femme de Venise*); nine of the plaster figures were later cast in bronze.[39]

In other words, any single shot of a *Woman of Venice* sculpture is a frame of a long take, none of the women is any more 'finished' than the other, and there is no prescribed order to how the individual women should be positioned in the collective sculpture, especially if one considers that the women were possibly renumbered after the casting. What further complicates the matter is that there exist different versions of the working process of these individual figures and of their exhibition and casting history. Each sculpture can be seen as a transposed motif of the other, but in a somewhat uncanny manner because there is neither an original motif nor a visually proportionate re-presentation of a single image despite their apparently sharing the same mass and process of creation.

In their perfect alignment of standing apart, the *Women of Venice* sculptures attain an air of solidarity in their implied spaces that interweave with the gaps of actual exhibition space in between. Here, the conjunction of the implied and actual space is not merely concentrated or reduced, but temporized with the duration of the work-in-progress and the stasis of the work-as-exhibited. Because of this, the form of solidarity perceived in *Women of Venice* is an assertion of solitude that is unitary but not unified; by conflating the individual frames of the sculpture with its collective frame, Giacometti inserted duration into repetition and created human figures that appear to be concentrated, minimized, yet disintegrating.

By the 1960s, and especially in the last three years of his life, Giacometti was largely creating busts that achieved a stronger sense of visual solidity especially in the face and head, even though the same unfinished, knobbly texture still marked the texture of the torso. According to Hohl, it is in these late bronze busts that

Giacometti 'made the art object into a subject' by depicting a strong, unflinching gaze that, in its 'act of looking', supplanted the body of the portrait:

> The act of looking is the subject's most succinct expression of being alive, for it involves the whole head and the whole upper body, while the eyes, the pupils, are only gristly lumps or vague recesses. The more the presentation of the body and the shoulders is fragmented, in the very last works, the stronger is the impact of the bust as a subject.[40]

The act of looking that comes across in these late busts is a combination of a few elements that have independently been explored in earlier sculptures, but never within the same work: first, the impression of a directed gaze by working through the area surrounding the eye sockets and the nose; second, the head as the central axis of perspective by detailing the face and slightly elongating the neck in proportion to the head and torso; and third, the body as receding in importance and spatial grounding by leaving it fragmented, roughly knobbled, and acting in part as a stand for the bust. In effect, these busts achieve a wavering sense of visual solidity and spatial dissolution due to the fragmentation of the torso and the implied weight of the head. This implied weight of the head supports the face which, in turn, frames the gaze and stages the act of looking. In other words, Giacometti utilized scale and frame not just to manipulate spatial perceptions between the viewer and the figure, but also to direct those perceptions of distance and distancing that occur in the reading of the figure itself.

This act of looking in the late busts can be seen more clearly when briefly compared with three other sculpted heads and busts of Diego from the 1950s to the 1960s. Notice that there is an increasing sense of frontality in these sculptures. In *Man with Windbreaker* (1953), the wide, enlarged frame of the body gathers the weight of the sculpture and generates a presence of depth in the figure that extends into a sense of three-dimensionality beyond the face or the head. This is conceptually inverted in *Large Thin Head* (1954) where the blade-like head compresses depth into surface and demands the viewer move around the figure to reconstruct its face almost as a faciality-in-progress — the face in its totality can neither be perceived frontally, nor in profile, but only in the viewer's process of looking while moving around it.[41] *Head on Base* (1958) gives a strong sense of staging the face not just due to the clear demarcation of figure and base, but also to the almost-equal proportion of figure to base. This elevates, separates and isolates the head from its implied space, effectively projecting it as a figure of monumentality into the actual exhibition space. The visuality of the sculpture here is one that approaches iconography: in its overt staging within actual space, the face in looking ahead calls for a thematic, artistic or symbolic recognition rather than a realistic identification. It is only in the late *Bust of Diego* (1964) that the frontality of the sculpture coalesces with the weight and gaze of the figure from within and into a space that is both implied and actual; the most significant factor that constitutes this effect is the act of looking derived from a combination of the three aforementioned factors.

These elements are further developed in the late bronze busts of Annette and Eli Lotar towards residual figuration. In particular, their acts of looking interrogate certain aspects of distance and distancing that can be drawn in close comparison to the figure of Joe in Beckett's *Eh Joe.*

Looking as Searching and Retrieving

A striking feature of Giacometti's late busts, most notably those of Annette, is the slight leaning forward of the figure. In *Bust of Annette IV* (see figures 1.4 and 1.5) and *Bust of Annette VIII*, the head projects from the frame of the body due to the arching forward of the neck, as can be clearly observed in the side profiles of the sculptures. Giacometti creates the act of looking by sculpting the posture of looking; in the slight reaching forward of the head, Annette appears to be looking for something, or looking at something attentively. But this is a posture of looking that is more likely implied than actual, as Giacometti's sitters usually sat in an upright, relaxed posture rather than one that was forward-leaning and slightly hunched (see fig. 1.6).

In other words, Giacometti extends the act of looking into a looking-at or looking-for by sculpting the compression of that distance in one's looking closer; the act of looking becomes a retrieval of proximity and a recovering of nearness. The displacement of the actual space in the bust's leaning forward creates the illusion of reducing the distance between the subject's position of looking and the object being looked at more closely. In effect, Giacometti sculpts the negative space of the act of looking itself into the sculpture, by displacing actual physical space into implied visual space.

But more than that, for the bust in its enacted posture of looking closer also reflects our very posture of observation in the actual space of the museum. A case in comparison would be the much earlier sculpture *Gazing Head* (1928), which Giacometti had sculpted with the intention of recreating 'the sensation of a face seen from very near'.[42] Here, the perception of nearness is conceptualized rather than enacted: the impression of seeing closely finds its reflection in the physical dents, also impressions, of the sculpture. Like many surrealist or cubist sculptures, the title of the work cues our direction of looking. In this sculpture, our search for the gaze is found, rather than reflected, in the fragment of a face in which an eye appears to sit embedded. The work becomes a glance of nearness rather than a process or posture of looking closely. Sylvester even suggests that this could be an intimate gaze:

> Of someone very close to one, at a point at which one is gazed at only by a lover, or in infancy was gazed at by one's mother, when just a part of the other's face — an eye and a cheek and part of the nose — fills the field of vision.[43]

In this respect, Giacometti sculpts nearness as the face-seen in *Gazing Head* rather than in a seeing-face as in the *Annette* busts.[44]

On the other hand, what we observe in the last bust of Eli Lotar (see figure 1.7) is a posture of looking back rather than a looking-for or looking-at. The sculpture's head is in line with the rest of the body, and the melding of the enlarged hands and arms into the base of the sculpture gives the figure a sense of weight and stability that suggests rapt attention and inertness. This impression of a gaze that receives or

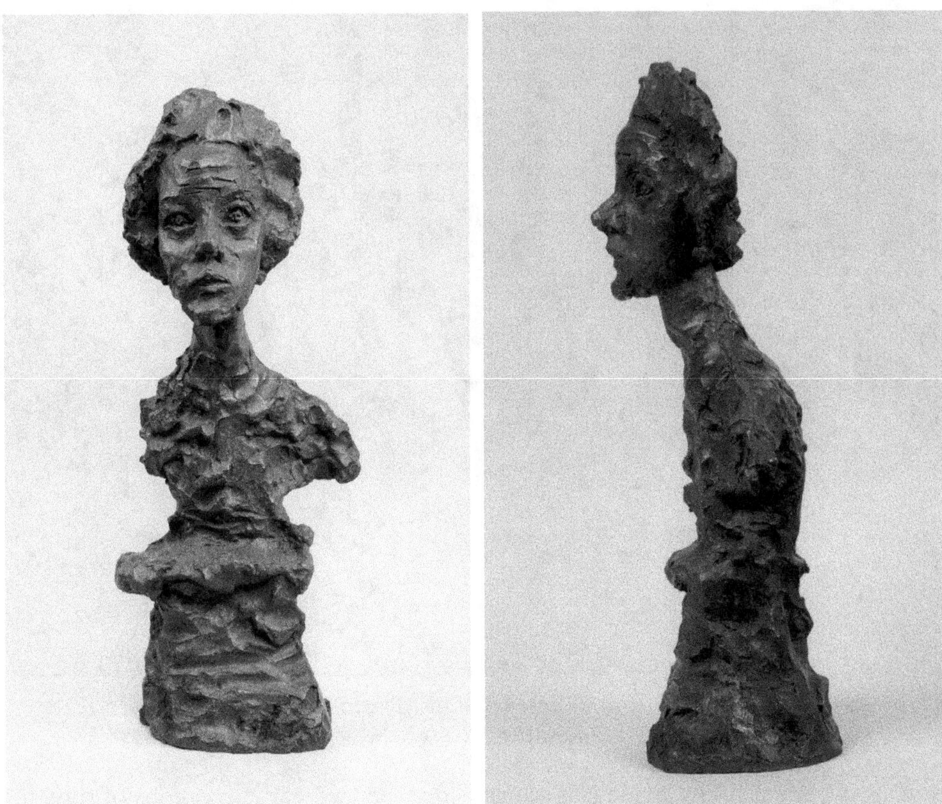

Figs. 1.4 amd 1.5. Alberto Giacometti, front and profile views of *Bust of Annette IV*, 1962, bronze, 58.4 × 23.7 × 20.3 cm, Alberto and Annette Giacometti Foundation, Paris.

Photo credit: Fondation Giacometti, Paris.

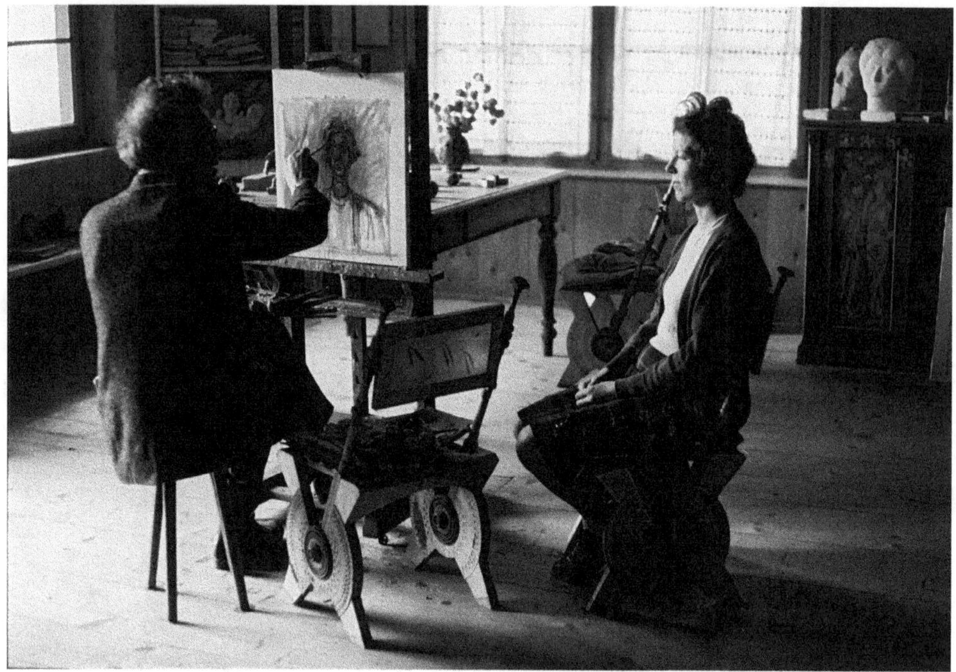

Fig. 1.6. Ernst Scheidegger, photograph of Alberto and Annette Giacometti in Stampa, 1965. © 2020 Stiftung Ernst Scheidegger-Archiv, Zurich.

returns is perhaps more evident if we consider the two earlier versions of the bust of Lotar that Giacometti sculpted. In *Head of Man (Lotar I)* (1965), the gaze is not supported by the posture of the body and assumes the weight of the figure as an act of active looking. This becomes slightly more diffuse in *Bust of Man (Lotar II)* (1964–65), where the relaxed posture anchors the gaze, even though the rest of the body is given so little definition that the sculpture appears more perceptual than physical.

It is only in the last bust of Lotar, *Lotar III*, that the gaze of the sculpture appears to have been returned before it is given; this is what gives it the impression of being a subject of looking-back rather than a process of looking-at. According to Sylvester, Lotar had sat for Giacometti close to four hundred times from the end of 1963 for these three busts, the last of which was still in progress when Giacometti died in January 1966.[45] Lotar turned out to be Giacometti's 'ideal model' due to his absolute immobility. According to Giorgio Soavi, 'he didn't breathe, he didn't think, he remained focused on the highest point'.[46] For Giacometti, the coalescence between the transmission and the translation of the act of looking seems to have been the most acute from a living body that appeared otherwise to be the most inert. In the last bust, this inertness is given to us as fixation: first, in the sinking and accumulation of the frame of the body into the ground (this is especially evident in the profile view of the sculpture, which shows a triangular coagulation of bronze merging the lower arms with the legs and back, hence giving the impression of

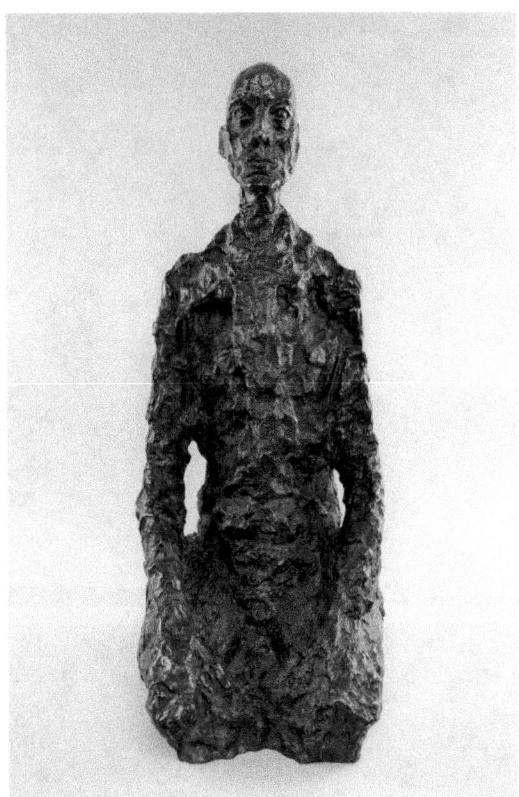

Fig. 1.7. Alberto Giacometti, front and profile views of *Bust of Man Seated (Lotar III)*, 1965–66, patinated bronze, 65.5 × 28.2 × 35.5 cm, private collection.

Photo credit: Fondation Giacometti, Paris.

Lotar kneeling and being anchored downwards); and second, in the coarse yet defined rigidity of the frame in supporting the head as 'a prop for the gaze' — this impression of being propped upwards is further intensified by Lotar's slightly upward tilt of the head.[47]

At this point, it is worth noting that *Lotar II* and *Lotar III* stand out in Giacometti's post-1950 *œuvre* as busts that extend in frame, approaching those of half-figures. After the group compositions of 1950, Giacometti produced many more busts than figures, especially where male portraits were concerned, because he felt a need to concentrate on the head. In his 1964 interview with Sylvester, he said that he had not sculpted a nude from life 'for nearly ten years' and was 'looking forward to starting again' but this time with less 'substance'.[48] What makes *Lotar III* particularly special is the increased definition of the frame from which the arms and thighs can be distinguished; this is also seen in *Half-length of a Man* (also called *Diego Seated*) made at the same time, but is mostly not evident in the other late busts. The stretched fixation of the frame — a sculptural turn of the word 'fixation' originally

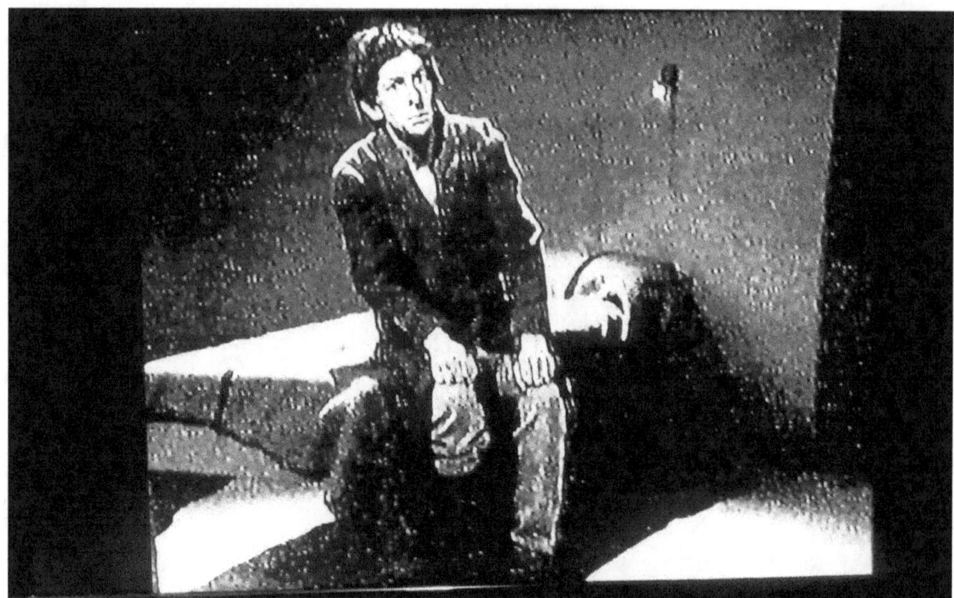

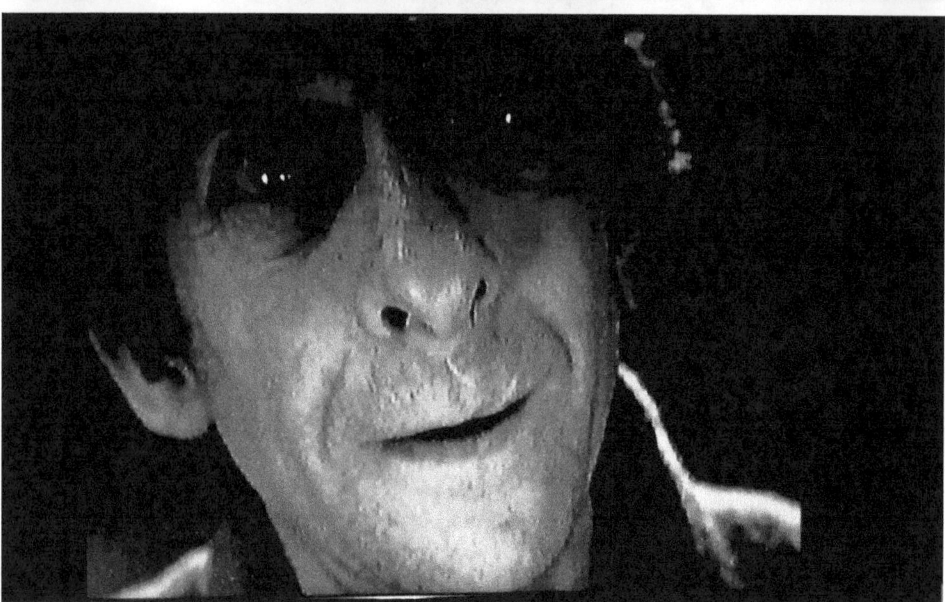

FIG. 1.8. Frame when woman's voice first begins in *Eh Joe* (BBC, 1966), featuring Jack MacGowran as Joe and Siân Phillips as voice.[51]
FIG. 1.9. Last frame of *Eh Joe* (BBC, 1966).

used to denote the alchemical process of reducing a volatile essence to a permanent, material form — temporally and spatially grips the open, horizontal stare of Lotar, thus re-locating the gaze back upon himself rather than at an object exterior to him. *Lotar III* retrieves the act of looking back upon the seer as subject; nearness becomes a return to the self rather than a reflection of the other.

This act of looking as searching and retrieving can also be observed in the figure of Joe in Beckett's *Eh Joe*. For a start, the edging forward of the camera, by way of nine camera moves by 'four inches each time', allows the viewer to look at Joe's face increasingly closer until the camera moves so close by the last frame that it can no longer capture the entire frame of the face (see figures 1.8 and 1.9).[49] The camera moves not only cue the viewer's focus and direction of looking but also the intensity of the look: in framing Joe's face increasingly tightly, the camera gives no further access to Joe's movements and posture, and forces the viewer into a shallow, circumscribed bracket of looking. But there is, in fact, very little to be seen; Joe's face is supposed to be 'practically motionless throughout, eyes unblinking during paragraphs [and] impassive except in so far as it reflects mounting tension of *listening*'.[50] In other words, it is Joe's act of listening that the viewer is led to look at increasingly closely. This leading inwards as a form of cinematic narrative focalization, paradoxically, does not allow any further understanding of or identification with the subject targeted because there are no visual changes to be observed. The viewer, in being led from looking at Joe's entire frame in spatial depth to Joe's impassive face almost pressed upon the lens, goes from a looking-at to a looking-on. The cinematic zoom-in here, in fact, does the opposite of character identification or understanding because the lack of visual changes heightens the shallow field of vision and makes Joe's face mostly surface, pictorial and flat.

The viewer's process of looking thus mimics what the woman's voice terms as a 'starting in on'.[52] According to Voice, there are three subjects who have 'started in on' Joe: his father, who 'started in on [him] one June night and went on for years' before Joe was able to 'throttle him in the end'; the woman herself, who started in on him with 'normal strength'; and his Lord who might start in on him when he's 'done with [himself]'.[53] All who start in on Joe speak to him relentlessly until reduced to a whisper (the 'odd word') which finally 'stops in the end' or, as corrected by Voice, is stopped in the end by Joe by way of a 'mental thuggee'.[54]

What these subjects-turned-voices do to Joe or make Joe do to them is suggested, but where they come from and reside is obscured. As taunted by Voice, Joe seems to assume that they come from 'that penny farthing hell [he] call[s] [his] mind', and they continue 'behind the eyes', or in his head, and are things '[he] can't catch' ('on and off') but are squeezed 'in the brain'.[55] What complicates this positioning of Voice is its relationship with the camera movement. Since the only frame of reference for the camera movement is the temporary ceasing of Voice in between — 'when perhaps Voice has relented for the evening' — the viewer is led to associate the moving-in of the camera with the imminent closing-in of Voice, which like Joe's mother when 'her hour came', is also watching Joe at the same time that it speaks to him.[56] Indeed, Voice appears to be watching Joe from a position that he cannot access; this allows voice to taunt him with threats and questions such as 'there might be a louse watching you' or 'why don't you put out that light?'[57]

The viewer's act of looking, then, begins with a looking-at and ends with a looking-on as cued by the zooming-in of the camera. This process of looking into depth and a resulting withdrawal onto surface mimics Voice's 'starting in on' by way of a relentless speaking going on in him or speaking to him, and a simultaneous watching over him from an obscure location. But there remains a third crucial act of looking that is not covered, and it comes from the eyes that the viewer is increasingly directed to examine: is Joe looking? And if he is, what kind of a looking is it? Is he looking at someone, or back at someone, or for something, or simply looking into nothing? Or do his eyes stand for introspection? Here I suggest that Joe's looking is an act of retrieval in the form of remembering. The ten frames we have in *Eh Joe* are transposed portraits of remembering that project duration without chronology, hence recalling the *Women of Venice* sculptures made up of ten independent but mutually reflexive figures.

Retrieving as Remembering, Remembering as Receding

Joe's portrait of remembering comprises three strands of retrieving: Voice's recounting, the camera's repeating and the face's receding. In all three strands, and especially in Voice's recounting, the movement and effect of the 'starting in on' create a form of duration similar to an ebb and flow, or a come and go, or indeed an 'on and off' that Joe 'can't catch'. The interaction of these three strands enacts the process of remembering as a kind of ghostly claustrophobia; as the camera advances forward in a linear fashion, Voice relapses into a vortex of narratives that re-surface old faces and words, thus rendering Joe's face — and eventually just his gaze — both the elusive centre and the eventual target of the spiral and the line.

Let us now take a closer look at how Voice creates a sense of remembering. Throughout the play, Voice alternates between taunts at Joe, pieces of narratives and various repeated phrases. In the first four frames, Voice mainly taunts Joe with rhetorical questions such as 'What's wrong with that bed, Joe?' or 'Anyone living sorry for you now?', and only drops narrative scraps and jibes about her past relationship with Joe (frame 2), his throttling of his parents (frame 3) and the woman who visits him on Saturday (frame 4). Voice then resuscitates the narrative about herself in the fifth frame, and it is the first sustained recount that is not punctuated by repeated phrases or taunts at Joe. In this frame, the viewer is offered a glimpse into a younger Joe who had 'a powerful grasp of language' and spent summer evenings with Voice 'watching the ducks' and 'holding hands exchanging vows'.[58] Here we are offered a frame of looking into a time and space past, and it is through this that the face of Joe gains characterization and narrative.

But this is not to last, for Voice goes on to resuscitate her taunting of Joe, and repeats phrases from the earlier frames until the end of the play. Three particularly significant groups of phrases are 'It should be the best' (frame 5), 'The best's to come' (twice in frame 2, frame 8) and then 'You've had the best' (frame 10); then, 'When you're nearly home' (frame 5, 9), 'nearly home again' (frame 5); and finally,

'There was love for you' (frame 8) and 'There's love for you' (twice in frame 10). Not only is the viewer denied access to the narratives of Joe (which are only offered to us through the focalization of Voice), but she or he becomes increasingly aware of the processes used by Voice to compose the narrative as it become increasingly uneven and interrupted. In the constant submerging of the narrative of the past by the present (of stories with words, and face with voice, hence moving between Deleuze's 'languages' I, II and III) the viewer's act of looking into Joe is obliterated despite the repetitive and utterly mechanical inching ahead of the camera. The viewer goes nearer to him only to have his/her partial knowledge of him increasingly undercut and dissolved. Voice's recounting of stories amidst a web of repeated phrases thus works together with the camera's linear progression to give an effect of Joe's face receding despite the viewer getting closer, an effect that is analogous to our approaching Giacometti's *Grande Femme*, as discussed in the Introduction.

This receding is, in fact, visually enhanced in two ways: through the actor's involuntary expressions and reactions; and due to the low resolution of the final close-up images. In the 1966 BBC production, Joe's eyes shut forcefully in the last frame at the phrase 'gets out the Gillette' and they remain trembling closed for many seconds even though there is no such indication in the script.[59] At this point, it seems that Jack MacGowran, who had commented that shooting *Eh Joe* was the 'most gruelling 22 minutes [he had] ever had in his life', comes to the surface and swamps the face of Joe, thus interrupting the image of the face with yet another rupture of the present, this time as a strain of the un-choreographed performative.[60] Not only do the processes of looking occur within and between the implied space (both the diegetic, i.e. Voice and Joe, and the cinematographic, i.e. the movement of the camera), they interact with the actual act of looking (the audience watching the screens) and also revolve around the performer's own act of looking, who in retreating from the text, supplants Joe's face with his own. This is also observed in the 1972 UK production starring Patrick Magee, who allows tears to run down his face twice in the course of the text.[61]

The second visual factor that enhances this receding of the face is the grainy nature of the close-up shots in the last frames, due to the low resolution of the images produced on the television screens of the 1960s and 70s. In getting closer, Joe's face begins to break down into disparate, pixelated particles and the impression of the face (on top of its already being cut out of the frame in the last few camera movements) becomes less cohesive as a whole. This effect is, no doubt, enhanced by the quality of the television screens and the distance from which the audience would have been watching them. The protrusion of the slightly convex screen might have resulted in cast reflections and refraction of light, further obliterating the clarity of the image produced.

It is, therefore, uncanny that it is only in the last frame, when the camera is in this way too close, that the longest sustained narrative from Voice is given to the viewer before it too is obscured to a barely perceptible whispering wherein only selected words can be fully deciphered. In the receding of Joe's face into its own nearness, the face of the woman — 'in the wash', 'a few feet from the tide' and then 'in the stones' — washes up like an apparition that is neither completely dead nor present.[62] This ghostly impression is largely a result of the reminder of the woman's eyes, which was the opening description of the woman given by Voice in frame 8, and then mentioned again in the last frame:

> But there was one didn't... You know the one I mean, Joe... The green one... The narrow one... Always pale... The pale eyes... Spirit made light... To borrow your expression... The way they opened after... Unique... Are you with me now?... Eh Joe?... There was love for you. (Frame 8)
>
> Scoops a little cup for her face in the stones... The green one... The narrow one... Always pale... The pale eyes... The look they shed before... The way they opened after... Spirit made light... Wasn't that your description, Joe? (Frame 10)[63]

As Joe's gaze becomes obscured in extreme nearness, that of the woman begins to emerge from remembering's distance. The close detailing of her eyes opening 'after-' projects the initiation of a gaze of whose time, place and recipient we are not able to know. The gaze opens and lingers, and indeed lingers on with Voice who only whispers clearly the following words, which stand out from other words 'almost inaudible', towards the end of the play: 'imagine-stone-'Joe Joe'-stones-lips-Imagine-solitaire-stone-eyes-Breasts-hands-Imagine-stones-There's love for you-Eh Joe?-Eh Joe?'.[64] Of these words, 'solitaire' and 'breasts' have never before been mentioned by Voice, and they prick the soundscape in its repetitive lull and apparent fading away. Yet, this is a fading away that happens because Voice, like the face, has come close enough for us to hear its whisper.

In this last frame, we have an intercalated sense of compression not just in the act of looking but also in the act of listening. In the trudging forward of the camera, the emerging of the woman's face and the leaning-in of Voice's whisper, Joe's static, receding face becomes a portrait of remembering that is at once claustrophobic and vacuous. His gaze becomes an act of looking because it gains a posture of remembering. In its final compression against the screen, Joe's gaze can no longer travel outwards because it has no space to travel forth. Remembering as an access to memory is denied in this final portrait of optical and aural compression, which becomes at once haunting and intimate in its pictorial flatness (here, one recalls Mathews' discussion of photographic reproductions of *Gazing Head* which deny our access to the pencil marks on the reverse surface of the sculpture). In this respect, nearness becomes a confrontation of proximity and obliteration. *Eh Joe* in its residual figuration enacts remembering as an act of looking that is eventually denied its gaze both forward and backward.

The Gaze is Also Denied

While Joe's gaze gains its fixation from the immobility of the face and the stasis of the voice and camera over the duration of the work (a portrait of portraits-in-progress, as it were), the gaze in Giacometti's late busts confronts us in its immediacy and entirety at first sight. However, what makes them similar is that their processes of depiction become increasingly present or visible in the course of viewing the works, which makes the viewer conscious of his or her perspective on the works. We have already seen how Joe's gaze is made reflexive by the interaction of Voice's recounting, the camera's repetition and the factors of performance contributing to the receding of the face. In the case of the busts, it is the increasing explication of the distance between the bust and the viewer that makes its creative processes of omission and translation increasingly visible in the work.

The gaze of these sculptures places us in the same distance that separated Giacometti from his sitters. If indeed Giacometti has succeeded in sculpting the perception of remaining at a distance, then our position of viewing the sculpture is fixed in this implied space of receiving the image even as we move within the actual, shared space where the sculpture is placed. This would mean, as a consequence, that the fixation of the bust's gaze both locates and removes us because the bust irreplaceably projects the distance of vision between the sitter and Giacometti by replacing other versions of seeing. This is further complicated by the understanding that the distance of vision exists not in the realistic space between the artist and the sitter in Giacometti's studio, but in the projected space of Giacometti's looking at the sitter and the sitter looking back both in the studio and in his memory. In other words, when Giacometti sculpts Lotar both from life and memory — a practice of simultaneity he adopted because it opened up possibilities both for better seeing and for moving on with his work — he gives a singular vision by effacing other ways of seeing the object.

This working from life and memory is both synchronic and diachronic. After 1953, after having mostly worked only from memory from 1939, Giacometti tended to alternate rapidly between works of different media and sitters within any one stretch of time, or/and return to works from the past (sometimes years before) and modify them abruptly from memory even if they were originally modelled from life. This alternation helped him create new possibilities of representation across works:

> In working from life, you always see much more than you can cope with, so you get lost in too many complications. In working from memory, you try to retain what has struck you most forcibly. At the same time it helps you to go on working from life. Ultimately, my idea would be to work in exactly the same way whether from memory or from life — that the two should overlap completely. [...] That's why I always, or very often, work in parallel on the same head both from life and from memory. It always helps me. Or even if it's not the same model, even if it's two heads of two different people, one from memory and the other from life, it's exactly the same pursuit; I have to try to understand the same thing. And if I make some progress from memory, it opens up more possibilities when I'm working from life.[65]

This synchronic working of multiple pieces from both memory and life can be seen in relation to a more diachronic approach, which usually entails re-sculpting, from memory, past works that had been sculpted from life. This was the case for the Lotar busts, of which James Lord gives an account in *A Giacometti Portrait*:

> On one of the sculpture stands there was a large bust wrapped in plastic. Presently he began to remove this plastic, uncovering the rags underneath

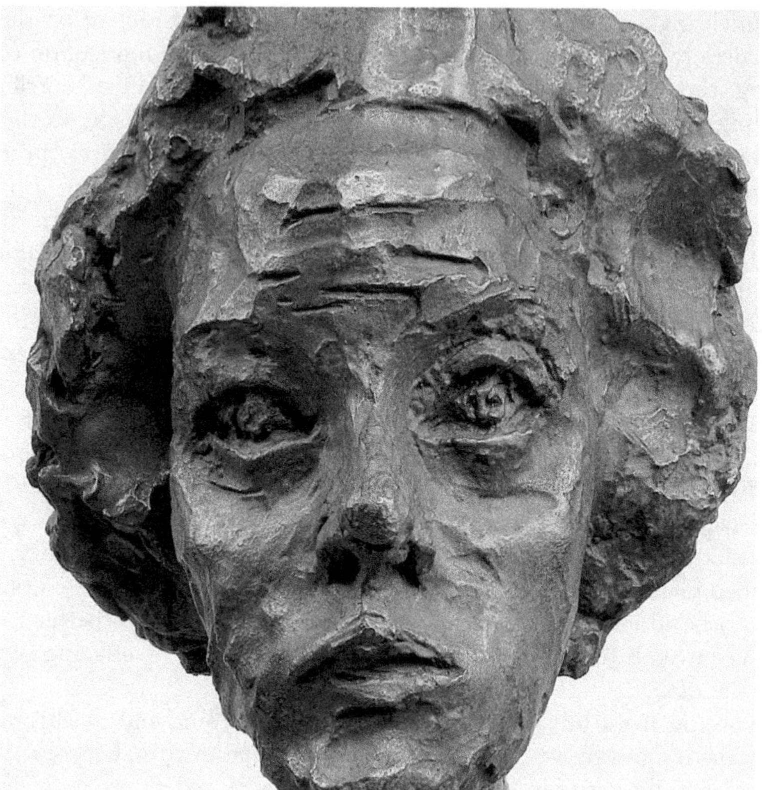

FIG. 1.10. Close-up image of *Bust of Annette IV*, 1962, bronze, 58.4 × 23.7 × 20.3 cm, Alberto and Annette Giacometti Foundation, Paris.

Photo credit: Fondation Giacometti, Paris.

> which he carefully unwound one after another and threw on the floor. It was like seeing a mummy being unwound after thousands of years. He was surprised and pleased to find to find that the rags were still damp, for it had been three months since he had worked on the bust, a portrait from life of a friend (Elie Lotar, the photographer). He then began to gouge and press and squeeze the clay so violently that several lumps of it dropped off onto the floor.[66]

In our accounting for these different versions of synchronic and diachronic seeing, the fixation of the bust's gaze thus necessitates omission and translates its being seen as subject. It is this being seen that lies at the crux of this translation. What we have here is translation as a phenomenology of seeing rather than a produced phenomenon of sight, much in the same way that translating a text from one language to another is, according to Clive Scott, largely concerned with translating the phenomenology of reading into a wholly new context.[67]

For Giacometti, what lies at the centre of this phenomenology of seeing is the encounter with the living gaze. This importance of the gaze can be understood through an incident that happened to him in the early 1920s when at art school:

> One day, when I wanted to draw a girl, something struck me, which was that I suddenly saw that the only thing that stayed alive was her gaze. Everything else — the head turning into a skull — came to more or less the same thing as a dead man's skull. What made the difference between a dead man and the person was her gaze [...]. It's not the imitation of an eye, it's purely and simply a gaze.[68]

Reproducing this encounter sculpturally begins with situating the busts in postures and positions that generate the impression of different forms of looking. As mentioned earlier, Annette's posture of leaning forward gives the impression of a gaze going outwards in search of an object, but Lotar's position of fixation retracts and anchors his gaze back upon himself, thus giving us the impression of a gaze that sees without looking at anything in particular. This is an interrogation of the Lacanian gaze that returns upon the seer as subject — the seer is *always already* seen in return by an invisible, anonymous agent.[69] In Giacometti's late busts, these postures and positions of seeing are inextricable from the sculptural construction of the eye, which creates the impression of the gaze. The eyes are where the greatest density and clarity of linear refinement gathers: the linear paths delineating the curve of the eye intersect and overlap closely, and usually appear sharper and at times more forceful (see figure 1.10).

However, observe that most of this linear work, which is very much in the style of a draughtsman, begins in the contour of the eye and radiates outwards and downwards towards the rest of the face; the eye itself is scantly worked on and the pupils are usually indicated with mere vertical strokes. The eye is constructed by a concentrated delineation of its position and a diffusion of this concentration outwards; when we read the face, these linear indentations actually direct our looking towards the blank centre of the eye. The impression of the gaze, then, is produced by way of a superimposition of these deictic, non-mimetic lines and our lines of perception. The lines that Giacometti sculpts away from the eyes lead our looking to their blank centres, which are filled in by our lines of perception in the act of looking.

It is by re-tracing Giacometti's lines of sculpting that we retrace Lotar's and Annette's gazes in their positions ultimately of lack. Here then, as in *Eh Joe*, the figure's gaze stands in as a kind of residual figuration that aligns remembering as both a process of creating and an act of looking — at once arduous and instinctive, diffusive and targeted.

Notes to Chapter 1

1. Aulus Gellius, *Attic Nights*, trans. by John Carew Rolfe, 3 vols, Loeb Classical Library (Cambridge, MA: Harvard University Press, 1927), II, 229.
2. *Shades: Three Plays by Samuel Beckett*, dir. by Donald McWhinnie and Anthony Page, *The Lively Arts* (BBC2, 1977).
3. For example, see Stanton B. Garner, 'Visual Field in Beckett's Late Plays', *Comparative Drama*, (1987), 349–73; Erik Tonning, *Samuel Beckett's Abstract Drama: Works for Stage and Screen, 1962–1985* (Bern: Peter Lang, 2007); Catharina Wulf, *The Savage Eye/ L'Œil fauve: New Essays on Samuel Beckett's Television Plays* (Amsterdam: Rodopi, 1995); Martin Esslin, 'A Poetry of Moving Images', in *Beckett Translating/ Translating Beckett,* ed. by Alan W. Friedman, Charles Rossman

and Dina Sherzer (University Park: Pennsylvannia State University Press, 1987), pp. 65–76; Jonathan Kalb, 'The Radio and Television Plays, and "Film"', in *The Cambridge Companion to Beckett,* ed. by John Pilling (Cambridge: Cambridge University Press, 1994), pp. 124–44.

4. Samuel Beckett, *Quad et autres pièces pour la télévision, suivi de L'Épuisé par Gilles Deleuze,* trans. by Edith Fournier (Paris: Minuit, 1992); Gilles Deleuze, 'The Exhausted', *SubStance,* 24 (1995), 3–28. See for example, Mary Bryden, 'The Schizoid Space: Beckett, Deleuze, and "L'Épuisé"', *Samuel Beckett Today/ Aujourd'hui,* 5 (1996), 85–94; Lydia Rainford, 'How to Read the Image? Beckett's Televisual Memory', in *Literature and Visual Technologies: Writing after Cinema,* ed. by Julian Murphet and Lydia Rainford (Basingstoke: Palgrave Macmillan, 2003), pp. 177–96; Graley Herren, *Samuel Beckett's Plays on Film and Television* (New York: Palgrave Macmillan, 2007); Eckart Voigts-Virchow, 'Exhausted Cameras: Beckett in the Tv-Zoo', *Samuel Beckett: A Casebook,* 25 (1998), 225.
5. Deleuze, 'The Exhausted', p. 9.
6. Ibid.
7. Ibid., p. 12.
8. Ibid.
9. Ibid., p. 9.
10. Rainford, 'How to Read the Image', p. 179.
11. Bryden, 'The Schizoid Space', p. 89.
12. Peter Gidal, *Understanding Beckett: A Study of Monologue and Gesture in the Works of Samuel Beckett* (London: Macmillan, 1986), p. 94.
13. Mladen Dolar, *A Voice and Nothing More* (Cambridge, MA: MIT Press, 2006), p. 60. For acousmatic sound, see Brian Kane, *Sound Unseen: Acousmatic Sound in Theory and Practice* (Oxford: Oxford University Press, 2014); Michel Chion, *The Voice in Cinema* (New York: Columbia University Press, 1999).
14. On close-ups and theatre, see Gidal, *Understanding Beckett*, p. 95.
15. For 'Not I' and surrealism, see Enoch Brater, 'Dada, Surrealism, and the Genesis of Not I', *Modern Drama*, 18 (1975), 49–59.
16. Tubridy, 'Vain Reasonings', p. 114.
17. On Mouth and its rejection of positions of subjectivity, see Derval Tubridy, 'Vain Reasonings: Not I', in *Samuel Beckett: A Casebook,* ed. by Jennifer M. Jeffers (New York: Routledge, 2012), pp. 111–32. Also see Enoch Brater, 'The "I" in Beckett's Not I', *Twentieth-century Literature,* 20 (1974), 189–200.
18. For further reading, see Albert Abramson, *The History of Television, 1942 to 2000* (Jefferson, NC: McFarland, 2002); Rick Marshall, *History of Television* (New York: Gallery Books, 1986).
19. James Knowlson, *Damned to Fame: The Life of Samuel Beckett* (New York: Simon & Schuster, 1996), pp. 435–36.
20. For example, see Mary Ann Doane, 'The Close-up: Scale and Detail in the Cinema', *Differences: A Journal of Feminist Cultural Studies,* 14 (2003), 89–111; David Bordwell, Janet Staiger, and Kristin Thompson, *The Classical Hollywood Cinema: Film Style & Mode of Production to 1960* (London: Routledge, 1988).
21. All stills from *Shades* in this chapter are taken from a video recording of the broadcast accessed at the British Film Institute, London.
22. For the relation between music, narration and modernism, see Eric Prieto, *Listening In: Music, Mind and the Modernist Narrative* (Lincoln: University of Nebraska Press, 2003).
23. Stanley E. Gontarski, 'Revising Himself: Performance as Text in Samuel Beckett's Theatre', *Journal of Modern Literature,* 22 (1998), 131–45 (p. 142); Martin Esslin, 'Towards the Zero of Language', in *Beckett's Later Fiction and Drama: Texts for Company,* ed. by James Acheson and Arthur Kateryna (New York: St. Martin's, 1987), pp. 35–49 (p. 44).
24. This recording was made unknown to Beckett in Paris in 1987, and is now available at the Beckett Collection at the University of Reading (JEK C/2/1/4).
25. Martha Fehsenfeld, '"Everything Out But the Faces": Beckett's Reshaping of *What Where* for Television', *Modern Drama,* 29 (1986), 229–40 (pp. 233–34).
26. See Izaak Walton, *Walton's Lives of Dr. John Donne, Sir Henry Wotton, Richard Hooker, George*

Herbert, and Dr. Robert Sanderson, with Some Account of the Author and His Writings (Boston: William Veazie, 1865).
27. Fehsenfeld, '"Everything Out But the Faces"', p. 233.
28. Samuel Beckett, *Endgame*, in *The Complete Dramatic Works*, pp. 89–134 (p. 93).
29. Jean-Paul Sartre, 'The Quest for the Absolute', in *Essays in Aesthetics*, ed. and trans. by Baskin, pp. 99–108 (p. 106).
30. Ibid.
31. Jean-Paul Sartre, 'The Paintings of Giacometti', in *Essays in Aesthetics,* pp. 67–78 (pp. 69–74).
32. Cited in Sylvester, *Looking at Giacometti*, p. 143.
33. Ibid., p. 47.
34. Ibid., p. 143.
35. Ibid., p. 146.
36. Reinhold Hohl, *Alberto Giacometti* (New York: H. N. Abrams, 1972), p. 278.
37. Reinhold Hohl, 'Giacometti and His Century', in *Alberto Giacometti: Sculpture, Paintings, Drawings*, ed. by Angela Schneider (Munich: Prestel, 2008), pp. 45–51 (p. 49).
38. Sylvester, *Looking at Giacometti*, p. 149.
39. Reinhold Hohl, 'Chronology', in *Alberto Giacometti*, ed. by Schneider, pp. 7–43 (pp. 32–33).
40. Hohl, 'Giacometti and His Century', p. 50.
41. See Sylvester, *Looking at Giacometti*, p. 152. For a particularly illuminating reading of depth and flatness in this sculpture, see Mathews, *Alberto Giacometti*, pp. 180–84.
42. Sylvester, *Looking at Giacometti*, p. 42.
43. Ibid., p. 86.
44. Mathews draws our attention to the unseen or the obliterated in nearness by pointing out that photographic reproductions of sculpture head-on do not and cannot allow us to see what is on the back. In fact, Giacometti had made pencil marks on the back of the plaster version, and had even planned to create a back 'with facial features indicated in the same method and style, but using protrusions rather than indentations' in his preparatory study of the sculpture (*Alberto Giacometti*, pp. 177–79).
45. Sylvester, *Looking at Giacometti*, p. 132. When Diego travelled back to Paris from Chur on 12 January 1966 (the day after his brother passed away), he 'thawed out the rags wrapped around the clay figure of Eli Lotar and made a plaster cast of this last work'. The bronze version was subsequently placed on Giacometti's grave in the cemetery of San Giorgio in Borgonovo (Hohl, 'Chronology', p. 41).
46. Giorgio Soavi, as quoted in the 'Biography' section of Alberto and Annette Giacometti Foundation <http://www.fondation-giacometti.fr/en/art/16/discover-the-artwork/97/alberto-giacometti/> [accessed 4 June 2016]. Also see James Lord, *Giacometti: A Biography* (New York: Farrar, Straus & Giroux, 1985).
47. Sylvester, *Looking at Giacometti*, p. 44.
48. Ibid., p. 226.
49. Samuel Beckett, *Eh Joe*, in *The Complete Dramatic Works*, pp. 359–68 (p. 361).
50. Ibid., p. 362.
51. Samuel Beckett, *Eh Joe*, dir. by Alan Gibson (BBC, 1966), 19:00 (all stills taken from a recording of the video at the British Film Institute).
52. Beckett, *Eh Joe*, in *The Complete Dramatic Works*, p. 363.
53. Ibid., pp. 363, 364.
54. Ibid., pp. 364, 363.
55. Ibid., pp. 362, 363, 364.
56. Ibid., pp. 362, 363.
57. Ibid., p. 362.
58. Ibid., p. 363.
59. Ibid., p. 366.
60. Knowlson, *Damned to Fame*, p. 478.
61. Samuel Beckett, *Eh Joe*, dir. by David Clark (University of London Audio-Visual Centre, 1972).
62. Beckett, *Eh Joe*, in *The Complete Dramatic Works*, p. 366.

63. Ibid., pp. 365, 366.
64. Ibid., pp. 366–67.
65. Sylvester, *Looking at Giacometti*, p. 226.
66. James Lord, *A Giacometti Portrait* (London: Faber & Faber, 1981), p. 5.
67. See Clive Scott, *Literary Translation and the Rediscovery of Reading* (Cambridge: Cambridge University Press, 2012), and *Translating the Perception of Text: Literary Translation and Phenomenology* (Oxford: Legenda, 2012).
68. Sylvester, *Looking at Giacometti*, p. 44.
69. Here I refer very broadly to Lacan's *Seminar X* in which he distinguishes concrete objects from *a* objects; the latter belong to an outside and are not objects of exchange. Llewellyn Brown's *Beckett, Lacan and the Gaze* (Stuttgart: ididem, 2019) offers an especially comprehensive treatment of Lacan's gaze in Beckett's works.

CHAPTER 2

❖

Lines in *Play*, *Come and Go* and *Paris sans fin*

> I have heard that the ancient Greeks wore a ring on the finger of the left hand which is next to the little finger. They say, too, that the Roman men commonly wore their rings in that way. Apion in his *Egyptian History* says that the reason for this practice is, that upon cutting into and opening human bodies, a custom in Egypt which the Greeks call ἀνατομαί, or 'dissection', it was found that a very fine nerve proceeded from that finger alone of which we have spoken, and made its way to the human heart; that it therefore seemed quite reasonable that this finger in particular should be honoured with such an ornament, since it seems to be joined, and as it were united, with that supreme organ, the heart.
>
> — Aulus Gellius, *Attic Nights*, Book 10[1]

As seen in the previous chapter, scale and frame play a crucial role in shaping the spatial perceptions of figures in televisual and sculptural media, but their roles in theatre and two-dimensional visual art are rather different and comparatively more restricted. The mimetic space of the stage eliminates direct scaling and focalization of the human figure by way of movement and magnitude (in comparison to a camera's zoom-in and close-up, for instance), and the frontal, framed canvas of a painting or a drawing likewise delineates a circumscribed space of representation which removes the viewer's direct investigation of and participation in the implied space of the figure. However, both Beckett and Giacometti made use of such restrictions to break down mimetic spaces themselves and the figures represented in them.

In Beckett's theatre, and especially the dramaticules, the onstage space undergoes modulation even if the action or dialogues remain largely static or similar throughout the play. For example, as mentioned in the Introduction, Listener and Reader in *Ohio Impromptu* seem to occupy a space that is catching up with, being caught up with, or paradoxically exceeded by the space evoked in the lines that Reader reads off, while W in *Rockaby* appears to be rocking in a dark space that gradually takes on the shape of the rocking to 'rock her off'.[2] In Giacometti's series of lithographs *Paris sans fin*, interior and exterior spaces, such as the studio and the Parisian streets, are populated by human figures so rapidly drawn and unconcealed in depiction that they look like linear filaments; some of these merge into the architecture rendering the entire setting elastic and transparent, while others emerge from blank pages, modifying neutral negative space into place, surface and texture. Hence, what feature more prominently in these prints, drawings and works for theatre are lines and linear forms, and especially the ways in which they transfer and translate narratives that refer back to the mimetic space of the figures. Such references usually evoke other diegetic or deictic elements of depiction which are themselves frequently linear too, such as stage directions in the dramatic texts and lithographic errors in printing. Reading the figures in these works therefore requires seeing, hearing and interpreting between both visual and non-visual lines, at times even reading more lines between and beyond those given. The line becomes an entity that shapes, makes and produces the figures in these works, but at the same time, it destabilizes the spaces from which these figurations emerge, thus unmaking the figures and rendering them residual figurations.

Two useful ways of conceptualising the line as an entity that makes and unmakes figures in theatre and drawing can be derived from Tim Ingold's anthropological account *Lines: A Brief History* and Merleau-Ponty's essay 'L'Œil et l'esprit' [Eye and Mind].[3] Ingold categorizes lines into three types: threads, traces and ruptures. Threads are filaments such as a necklace, the yarn of a ball of wool or the needles of a conifer. They 'may be entangled with other threads or suspended between points in three-dimensional space' but they are not drawn on surfaces, even if they have their own surfaces at a microscopic level.[4] The making of threads, such as threading or knotting, forms an ancient human art closely associated with the dexterity and precision of the hands and their grip. Elizabeth Wayland Barber argues that stringing forms the basic motivation for many grasping or connecting actions such as catching, carrying, holding and binding, and David Turnbull extends from this in suggesting that stories, strings and trails were possibly produced contemporaneously through close associations with narrative, journeying and weaving.[5]

This is particularly interesting when we consider the highly precise walkers that pervade the works of Beckett and Giacometti. Some examples include Watt's 'way of advancing' by simultaneously flinging out his leg and turning his chest in opposite directions,[6] or in *...but the clouds...* M's advancing of 'five steps' to and fro across the empty set after having 'walked the roads since break of day'[7] and Giacometti's *Piazza* (or sometimes titled *La Place*) comprising one standing woman and four walking men poised to take different trajectories towards the centre of the base, which in turn recall the walkers of *Quad* who avoid the centre of the stage.[8] What is of interest here is how walking as a kind of linear enactment is frequently closely entwined with the production and erasure of the written and spoken lines of its narratives.

For instance, the steps of May in *Footfalls* interrupt, accompany and generate the lines spoken by V and those upon which she herself seems to improvise. These steps disrupt the individual lines of the dialogue and monologues, and, in so doing, perpetuate the lines of the dialogue as monologue and vice versa. This walking is itself a rhythmic line constituted by the 'clearly audible rhythmic tread' of her steps, but it had not always been heard by the figures who populate the stories of May and V.[9] In V's narrative of May when she was 'still little more than a child', May had said, through V's voice, that 'the motion alone is not enough, I must hear the feet, however faint they fall'; in May's telling of the 'sequel', 'she' (who?) would walk at 'nightfall', 'up and down, up and down, that poor arm' of the 'little church' with 'no sound', 'none at least to be heard'.[10] Here the lines of audibility and movement diverge, but also the lines of the viewer's perception and the text's self-depiction: whose steps are we hearing and whence do they come?

This difficulty in locating presence amidst such linear displacements is heightened through May's last narrative about Amy: Amy, 'the daughter's given name, as the reader will remember', was heard by 'Old Mrs Winter, whom the reader will remember' saying 'Amen' at evensong even though Amy claims she 'was not there'.[11] May's diegetic move of referring to the 'reader' recalls the lines of the dramatic text, but these are lines that cannot be found because the names 'Mrs Winter' and 'Amy' have never been mentioned in the dramatic text of *Footfalls*. Perhaps the reader is supposed to look through Beckett's entire canon, or see 'Amy' in other names beyond the anagram of 'May'? What May evokes here is diegesis upon diegesis — the reader in flipping through, the viewer in trying to remember the printed words, and in both the attempt to make new lines of connection to fill in the gaps in given lines enact a kind of performative reading. This reading is performative because it interrupts itself, trails off into another kind of reading, fails to really find anything there, and brings back to the text only the movement of return or the gesture of having wandered. Steps enact such lines that move and move away; the reader or the viewer finds him or herself at once entangled in and displaced by this web of linear constructions. This mimics May's being cocooned in her wrap, itself a web of threads. For the 1976 Royal Court Theatre production in which Beckett directed Billie Whitelaw, this costume was created by Jocelyn Herbert from an old evening dress torn up with bits of cloth left 'to rag', and then imposed with pieces of shredded net curtain that Herbert dyed in 'different shades of gray', thus creating a costume that was a patchwork of depth and decay.[12] In this sense, May is not a figure wrapped in a web, but becomes herself unmade in this web of a figure, whose feet, as indicated by a stage direction, are hidden by the wrap.[13] As Gidal puts it, she is 'never a figure inside a wrap,' but is rather, 'as a whole a wrap', a wrap 'in toto'.[14]

The connection of threads to written and spoken lines moves us into Ingold's second class of lines as traces. Traces are marks that are 'left in or on a solid surface by a continuous movement', and are either additive or reductive depending on whether they superimpose an additional layer upon the surface, or score or scratch off the surface.[15] By this definition, crayon marks on paper are additive traces, but the marks left in the metal plate by an etching needle are reductive. According to Ingold, the verb 'to draw' refers to the 'activity of the hand both in the manipulation of threads and in the inscription of traces', and is not as readily distinguished from the verb 'to write' as is commonly held.[16] Etymologically, drawing (from Old English *dragan*) referred to the action of pulling or dragging a tool with one's hand across a surface, while writing (from Old English *writan*) referred to the incision of 'runic letters in stone', or more generally to the scoring or outlining of a figure or letter.[17] Hence, both words derive from the same action of the hand, with drawing emphasizing the manipulation of the tool (a kind of thread), and writing, the incised marks (traces) produced by the action:

> Thus one would *write* a line by *drawing* a sharp point over a surface: the relation between drawing and writing is here between the gesture — of pulling or dragging the implement — and the line traced by it, rather than, as it is conventionally understood today, between lines of fundamentally different sense and meaning.[18]

Given that writing was essentially a manipulation of threads into traces, it is not surprising that text (from Latin *textus*) referred to a thing that was woven, typically a cloth, and telling a story became known as spinning a yarn, and so on.[19] In this light, the word in both its vocal and written forms is fundamentally tied to the manipulation and conversion of threads and traces, and thus forms an integral and flexible element of the line, analogous to the point in visual art.

Many of Giacometti's drawings illuminate this flexibility of threads and traces, especially when they are drawn over surfaces which already have printed words on them such as postcards, envelopes and newspapers. For instance, in a drawing made on an envelope and dedicated to Giorgio Soavi, *Seated Women and Men's Heads*, four heads of different scales and profiles are enmeshed in a network of lines that overlap and envelop one another without a clear demarcation of space, depth or planar perspective.[20] Unlike Giacometti's portrait paintings, these heads are firmly depicted on the white surface as two-dimensional entities, and do not appear to recede into or emerge from the background. The materiality of the ink shows up as pathways of traces upon the white surface, creating an entanglement of lines that evoke in the white interstices of space in between the translucence of light upon skin, thread upon surface. In addition, the fraying lines from the heads make one wonder if they form the start or the end points of the drawing; if we follow the trails of these traces to their end, can we re-draw these heads from the beginning as our lines of perception? In juxtaposition to such a thought is the text that appears on the surface of the envelope belonging to multiple time-frames: the lines hand-written on the left-hand side at right-angles to the drawing seem to be addressed to Soavi and thus possibly written by Giacometti at the time of the drawing, while the remaining lines, including the words printed by an ink stamp on the right, appear to belong to the original text on the envelope. Following the trails of these lines gives us narrative in the form of transfer and address. Such traces and threads evoke different kinds of time and duration, and the ways in which they overlap and weave into each other frequently create new narratives or expose the existence of lines belonging to Ingold's third class, that of pre-existing ruptures in the surface.

Such ruptures as cuts, cracks and creases typically have the capacity to disrupt pre-existing lines and surfaces: cuts into grounds or materials tend to create new surfaces or divide pre-existing surfaces, cracks interrupt surfaces and the traces on them, and the pleats of a fabric or folds on a card are examples of creases that imbue the material with traces of a gesture or function.[21] Some ruptures are highly visible, such as cracks in the earth, but others such as contours or imprints of surfaces are not immediately apparent. For this reason, cuts and creases, while visible as natural phenomena, share many similarities with what Ingold calls 'ghostly lines', that is 'visionary' or 'metaphysical' lines frequently associated with abstract concepts and rationalization, including geometry and map contours.[22]

This interaction between lines of rupture and ghostly lines is productive for thinking comparatively about Giacometti's drawings and the diagrams to indicate the visual positioning and movement of the figures in the performance that Beckett included in the notes to many of his dramatic works.[23] These diagrams help the reader to visualize the stage in the theatre works or the camera shots in the television plays: the diagrams in *Ghost Trio* and *...but the clouds...* give the reader a clearer picture of how the figure appears on the screen. However, other diagrams give the reader an immediate visualization of the play that a viewer can only gradually acquire, or attempt to do so, as the play progresses: the diagrams for *Quad* form a case in point.

Quad differs from the other television plays in using only a single static 'raised, frontal' camera position and no other visual cinematographic effects (such as the blurring of the faces using gauze in *What Where*).[24] This appears to merge the static perspective of a theatre-goer with the unique spatial angle of the camera, in turn producing simultaneous effects of spectator engagement and distance that could begin to explain Beckett's insistence that *Quad* could not work on stage.[25] Broadly put, the play situates four 'players' within a geometrical system and manipulates their movements using arithmetic combinatorics.[26] The diagram that first appears in the dramatic text is immediately followed by corresponding text on the movements of the courses of action This allows the reader to imagine, in a single page, the course of action for the whole play. But the whole play *is* this action; the diagram is a kind of pre-text that gives the reader an overview of the action on fast-forward, but it is also a stage direction that realizes, in its entirety, the dramatic text. This alignment of figure and line, and the reader's realization of this from the start, is further complicated by the second diagram included towards the end of the dramatic text, which shows the deviations of movement from the original diagram due to Beckett's realization that E had become 'a danger zone' during its production in Stuttgart.[27] Together, the diagrams give the narrative of the text from depiction to perception and back to depiction. The reader of *Quad* thus imagines a play run on lines and its various permutations, combinations and alterations, but the viewer of *Quad* perceives figures walking, makes out that they are walking in some discernible linear pattern, and then realizes that the play does not seem to be going anywhere else. Thus, the lines of the diagrams made visible and invisible not only inform and organize the space and narrative of the text, but also disrupt the spatial and temporal positions of figure focalization for the reader and the viewer.

A comparison of these diagrammatic lines with Giacometti's technical drawing lines further shows how ghostly lines lead to those of rupture, but also how all three classes of lines have a tendency to translate into each other, giving the impression of the figure being made and unmade. In many of Giacometti's drawings, horizontal lines that traverse the face, body and background of figures all seem to refer to different degrees of invisibility. Some of those on the faces appear to be technical lines drawn to guide facial proportions and left unconcealed, those gently sketched in the background may be the contours of objects behind the figures and the strokes across the chest seem to be unintentionally deictic moves that undercut mimetic depth of the figure (these strokes also show up very often in the portrait paintings, and will be discussed in the next chapter). However, the lines of facial proportion also seem to overlap with the creases and wrinkles of the face, and the lines across the body could also be lines of light, vapour or texture. In these cases, technical ghostly lines of depiction show up as the unconcealed counterpart to threads and traces perceived through light, on the one hand emphasizing interruption, yet on the other evoking time, character and memory. Ingold's taxonomy shows that lines produce, modulate and erase figures in the form of movements and narratives. This is a dynamic interaction explored by both Giacometti and Beckett and which brings writing and drawing very closely together in text and performance.

From Ingold to Merleau-Ponty: Making and Seeing

Ingold's anthropological account gives a perspective of the line as both a product and process of different types of making, but in Merleau-Ponty's phenomenological approach, this making of the line is, first and foremost, considered a reversibility of seeing and being seen in 'the fabric of the world'.[28] Even though Cézanne is generally regarded as Merleau-Ponty's paradigm artist and Giacometti that of Sartre against the backdrop of existentialism, many of Merleau-Ponty's writings on painting and drawing are also useful for reading Giacometti's works, especially considering that Merleau-Ponty included Giacometti's works in his criticism, and Giacometti himself was influenced by both Merleau-Ponty and Sartre.[29] Written in 1960, 'Eye and Mind' extends from Merleau-Ponty's first two essays on painting, 'Le Doute de Cézanne' [Cézanne's Doubt] (1945) and 'Le Langage indirect et les voix du silence' [Indirect Language and the Voices of Silence] (1952), by proposing an ontology of reversibility and flesh through the perception of painting. According to this ontology, the body is an 'intertwining of vision and movement', which results in the realization that things perceived by the body are part of the world in which the body is itself caught up.[30] This world becomes 'an annex or prolongation' of the body which can only realize itself or come into being within, and as, such a material incrustation.[31] This relation between interiority and exteriority is a chiasmic one in which neither takes precedence, and it is this reversibility that, for Merleau-Ponty, situates vision as 'a thinking that unequivocally decodes signs given within the body' — what the viewer recognizes as resemblance in the exterior world is a 'result' of this perception from within, rather than a 'basis' for it.[32] It is on this point that Merleau-Ponty begins his investigation into depth as the first dimension of painting which, in its enfolding of length and width, becomes 'the experience of the reversibility of dimensions'.[33]

Merleau-Ponty included in the *Art de France* and Gallimard editions of 'Eye and Mind' two drawings by Giacometti — *Portrait d'Aimé Maeght* and another, untitled drawing for the frontispiece of an earlier work *Les Philosophes célèbres* — but did not comment in detail on the artist or his drawings. Of the remaining artists whose artworks he included in 'Eye and Mind', Matisse and Klee are the most directly referred to in the essay, and it is through these two figures that he proposes two distinct ways of 'freeing' the line and 'revivifying its constituting power'.[34] The first, through Klee, holds fast to creating an 'indirect', 'fundamental' or 'absolute painting' which 'renders' visible rather than imitates the visible; the painting is left to function freely and it is left to the title to designate 'the entity thus constituted' by the line.[35] The second, through Matisse, uses the line to constitute shapes not as 'physical-optical' representations, but as 'structural filaments' ('des nervures') which embody the force and inertia, and activity and passivity, of the entity represented.[36] The distinction lies in the mode of abstraction that the line harnesses in relation to visibility. In Klee, the line renders visible a form of vision that has no immediate external semiotic referent, whereas in Matisse the line shapes a vision that both identifies the external characteristics of the entity and embodies its 'hidden operations' from within. In both cases, the line is a certain 'disequilibrium' set upon the blank canvas, and it constitutes an emptiness that becomes the 'restriction', 'segregation', or 'modulation of a pregiven spatiality'.[37] This is how the line, according to Merleau-Ponty, is let free and enacts 'movement without displacement'; the line goes, making 'its way in space' and establishing a 'certain level or mode of the linear' that corrodes 'prosaic space'.[38]

Where do the lines of *Portrait d'Aimé Maeght* fit into this conception of line as movement and depth? In his analysis of the seven artworks that preface 'Eye and Mind', Glen Mazis suggests that Giacometti's lines are able to delineate the figure 'only by rendering outlines as moving, blurring, open to what is around them, as lines of force and ambiguity'; these lines are what draw us into the 'density' of the facial expression coming from within the figure of Aimé Maeght which is otherwise depicted as being 'solid', 'substantial' and 'reduced'.[39] This reading is supported by Brendan Prendeville, who argues that Giacometti can be seen to 'put vision into the visible' because the 'traces of the search are indistinguishable from the thing searched for'.[40]

Drawing from these interpretations, Giacometti's lines can, thus, be seen to take on certain characteristics within Merleau-Ponty's framework of line as movement and depth. While Giacometti's lines give the contour of a recognizably human figure, this contour is incomplete and diffusive. This gives the impression of a figure emerging into our vision, but also a figure that lends itself to the emergence of 'vision from within'. The figure of Maeght that the viewer perceives is thus a perception of depiction thrice over: it is the depiction of Maeght as seen by Giacometti, which is a visibility that depicts movement as vision from within, and this vision in turn depicts a being-caught-in-space as an ontology of reversibility and flesh. As such, the depicted line in Merleau-Ponty's ontology is always deictic and infinitely so. It is this chiasmic relation between perception and depiction that gives the line its multitude of meanings such as 'emptiness', 'movement', 'disequilibrium' and 'depth'.

The line that reverses seeing and being seen, according to Merleau-Ponty, is also that which makes its way across the surface of the paper, modifying the 'vacant background' into a 'spatiality' as in 'modern geometries'.[41] Here the ghostly line of Ingold's taxonomy creeps in. At the same time as the line translates vision into visibility and transforms surface into depth, it also ruptures existing lines and surfaces, or encourages us to read new ones between threads and traces both visible and non-visible. The line that 'goes' is also that which 'makes', 'unmakes' and 'remakes'; both the anthropological and phenomenological approaches provide a basis for analysing how lines translate and transform spaces, senses and narratives. These processes are central to the perception and depiction of figures in Beckett's works *Play* and *Come and Go*, and Giacometti's *Paris sans fin*. In particular, they generate several levels of invisibility in our reading of the figures through residual figuration.

Paris sans fin: An Inability to Return

Paris sans fin brings together 150 lithograph prints that Giacometti created between 1959 and 1965, and is an important work in the genre of the *livre de peintre* or *livre d'artiste*, loosely translated as an artist's book which contains illustrations printed exclusively by the artist rather than reproduced by technicians. Edited by Tériade, the 'grand instigator' of the *livre de peintre* in twentieth-century France, *Paris sans fin* was Giacometti's account of the Paris that he so loved;[42] in this respect it echoes Fernand Léger's *La Ville*, which had been dedicated to Paris and published by Tériade in 1959.[43] In a sequence noted by the artist at the foot of each illustration, *Paris sans fin* brings the reader through familiar spaces including the café, the train station, the artist's studio and the boulevards.

The crayon lines of the lithograph form the main type of linear trace in this book, but they are by no means the only type. Sixteen pages of the book were reserved for text written by Giacometti, only ten were filled, the remaining six pages being left blank in the posthumous publication of the book in 1969. The text was written in three phases from 1964 to 1965 after the images were completed and, together with the six blank pages, interrupt the sequence of paired prints thirteen times with no fixed pattern.[44]

However, that the written lines interrupt the drawn ones is not the impression that is formed at the start of the reading. The first ten lines of the text — in which Giacometti mentions the challenge of having to re-do thirty lithographs for the book in 1964 — precede plates 1 and 2 which show Parisian streets, and the text is only picked up again after plate 24, where it continues for two full pages. The turn of the page from written to drawn lines, from speech to vision, makes the viewer conscious of a change in modes of reading: instead of hearing a voice that gradually draws the reader into the verbal narrative that it is attempting to recount (it begins with 'fifteenth, no, sixteenth May 1964, in my room [...] I tried to resume, views of streets, interiors, it doesn't work anymore, where, how to resume?'),[45] the reader is now confronted with a 'meshwork' of lines already assembled, from which the reader has to make out where to start reading so as to place the elements of the visual narrative.[46]

This shift in the modes of reading is not merely a toggle of the senses involved in the experience of reading, but an interrogation of the senses involved in interpreting reading. This interpretation involves the assembling of narratives and narrativity. The reader first pieces together a verbal narrative from the written traces and, with the turn of a page, finds that the sentence she or he was expecting to be completed from the previous page has been interrupted with a different type of linear representation. This fracture silences; the printed traces no longer speak and the narrative ceases. However, this fracture also creates continuity: the translation of the written traces into drawn ones emphasizes the graphic dimension that they share.[47] The lithographic lines thus extend the graphic movement of the written lines through the space of the white pages, and it is this shared performance of the line that produces and provokes elements of narrativity in the print which in turn inform the words.[48]

This shift in modes of reading is further complicated by the insertion of the six blank pages. The first blank page appears beside plate 46, which shows us a streetlight and building. It is tempting to think of this blank as signalling a shift in focalization, since it precedes four pairs of interior spaces featuring his wife Annette, and is followed by a long sequence of exterior spaces (plates 46–98, interrupted by text four times).[49] However, the other five blank pages do not create the same effect. For instance, three of them appear consecutively beside plates 120 (landscape), 121 (very similar landscape) and 122 (female body with no indication of place), punctuating the visual narrative like gasps or pauses, on the one hand suggesting a temporal slowing-down or fast-forwarding analogous to a press of the button on the tape-recorder, and on the other mimicking instances when gaps show up in one's recollection and forgetting prevails. These blank pages thus inhabit, modify and rupture the verbal and visual narratives both diegetically and mimetically. In this sense they are analogous to Ingold's third class of lines, such as the pleats of a fabric or near-invisible creases on a surface.

Gaps in *Paris sans fin* show up not only as blank pages between verbal and visual lines, but also within the printed lithographic lines themselves due to the transfer lithographic process. Transfer lithographic lines are different from directly drawn lines because they are lines that are transferred not just once, as in traditional lithography, but twice: first from transfer paper to a zinc or limestone plate (by using water which dissolves the undrawn white surface of the transfer paper but not the greasy crayon lines); and then from this plate to paper. The result is an image that is neither drawn, nor painted, nor engraved, as described by Giacometti in the text placed between plates 24 and 25:

> Oh! l'envie de faire des images de Paris un peu partout, où la vie m'amenait, m'amènerait, la seule possibilité pour cela ce crayon lithographique, ni la peinture ni le dessin, ce crayon le seul moyen pour faire vite, l'impossibilité de revenir dessus, d'effacer, de gommer, de recommencer.[50]
>
> [Oh! the desire to create images of Paris a bit everywhere, where life would carry me, would take me, the only possibility for this lies in this lithographic crayon, neither painting nor drawing, the crayon is the only way to do it quickly, the impossibility of returning, effacing, erasing, restarting.]

This impossibility to return is temporal, spatial and material. When Giacometti writes of his desire to create images of Paris 'a bit everywhere' he could be referring to drawing images of Paris no matter where he is, or of a Paris which is itself 'all over the place', or of putting them everywhere (as in creating graffiti, scrawling on tablecloths, envelopes and scraps of paper). This is a drawing and re-drawing between image and after-image, sight and memory, visibility and non-visibility. The medium of transfer lithography adds another layer to this infinite blanketing of shifts between presence and absence, line and gap. Due to the doubled processes of transferring from transfer paper to metal plate and then to paper, most transfer lithographs present breaks or gaps in the lines of the final image, a consequence further exacerbated by the variable quality of transfer papers. This proved to be an obstacle for Giacometti when he tried printing the lithographs a second time in 1964, after a mock-up version had been first printed in 1961:[51]

> Giacometti subit ainsi un nouveau contretemps en découvrant en septembre 1964, devant des épreuves d'essai tirées par Mourlot, que le papier de certaines feuilles est trop vieux pour reporter convenablement le dessin. Contrairement à la pierre, ce papier n'admet pas les corrections, qui altéreraient sa surface préparée pour capturer les traits de crayon. Mais Giacometti veut précisément se soumettre à cette obligation d'aller droit au but, de tracer tout de suite l'image définitive: plus qu'une contrainte, elle est pour lui une libération, le promesse d'un travail rapide, léger, facile.[52]

> [Thus Giacometti suffered another setback upon discovering in September 1964, before the trial proofs printed by Mourlot, that the paper of some sheets was too old to properly transfer the drawing. Unlike stone, transfer paper does not allow corrections, which would alter the surface prepared to capture the crayon lines. But Giacometti wanted precisely to submit to this obligation of advancing directly towards the goal, of immediately drawing the final image: more than being a constraint, it is for him a release, the promise of a work that is rapid, lightweight, easy.]

That the paper was 'too old' is likely to mean that the drawing had been left on the transfer paper for too long: the earliest of these drawings were made in 1959 and most would have already been transferred once in 1961.[53] This gap between creation and repeated transfers could have affected the quality of the oil-based crayon marks, making it difficult for them to adhere to the metal plate upon the dampening of the transfer paper (a process which had already sacrificed one of Giacometti's drawings to water damage) and subsequently to be pressed onto paper.[54] In fact, imperfection seems ingrained into the very technique of transfer lithography from the start because transfer paper does not allow the use of the eraser, which Giacometti had increasingly integrated into his drawings from the mid-1950s.[55] But all these technical imperfections were, for Giacometti, a necessity born out of the need to produce what he saw immediately, without return, *sans fin*. The gaps in the lithographic lines present a sense of faithfulness to the history of production and the history of vision. They constitute marks of becoming that have, ironically, been rendered permanently and blankly visible to us due to the aging of time.

Finding the Female Figure Between Space and Light

Other than presenting various places in Giacometti's Paris, the prints also offer human figures in a variety of environments and situations. In particular, the female figure achieves a marked prominence as it appears in different settings of time and space, and in strikingly different postures from the majority who face front on in Giacometti's paintings, or stand immobile in his sculptures. For instance, Annette and Caroline are both depicted in profile (plates 41 and 51 respectively) and with their gaze away from Giacometti (plates 87 and 67) in interior and exterior settings, and a female figure appears to be dancing with a male in plates 145 and 146.

The frontispiece of the book presents an interesting case in point (see figure 2.1). It is a female nude in profile, seemingly caught in the movement of plunging forwards. The body exerts itself diagonally across the page, enacting both an extension and a fissure of the blank space. Its elongated frame pulls or stretches the white confines into its movement, while the truncation of both her legs and arms defines this movement as being caught in an interstice of time both before and after the plunge. The linearity of the contour is emphasized by swift, overlapping strokes, and is only briefly modulated by two bulges at the belly and the buttocks; the head, hair and breasts supplement this contour as haphazard curves, almost as interruptions to or protrusions of the figure. This figure is caught in movement amidst a completely empty setting, without contact with the ground or any other object, thus nudging it towards a gestural image which is purely bodily; yet this body has been deprived of most sense receptors, thus further reducing the bodily to the corporeal and inarticulate. It becomes an entity caught between contour and space, almost taking on the shape and pulse of a stream that flows and divides. The lines divide body and space, body from space, yet at the same time give body to space, and render body as space. To use the terminologies of Merleau-Ponty and Klee, the line corrodes space to render movement visible and to grasp it as visibility.

This rendering and grasping are exposed as linear texture, both as memory and by way of lithographic reproduction. The texture of the material lithographic line is superimposed with the texture of Merleau-Ponty's vision-as-ontology; in both, it is a texture of sensory and incomplete translation that emerges through the linear form. To get down to the specifics of Merleau-Ponty's argument, this 'texture' of visibility offers to the gaze 'traces of vision' so as to 'espouse' vision from within:

> The picture, the actor's mimicry — these are not devices borrowed from the real world in order to refer to prosaic things which are absent. For the imaginary is much nearer to, and much farther away from, the actual — nearer because it is in my body as a diagram of the life of the actual, with all its pulp and carnal obverse exposed to view for the first time. [...] And the imaginary is much farther away from the actual because the painting is an analogue or likeness only according to the body; because it does not offer the mind an occasion to rethink the constitutive relations of things, but rather it offers the *gaze* traces of vision, from the inside, in order that it may espouse them; it gives vision that which clothes it within, the imaginary texture of the real.[56]

A painting is therefore a visible rendering not just of vision, but of the texture

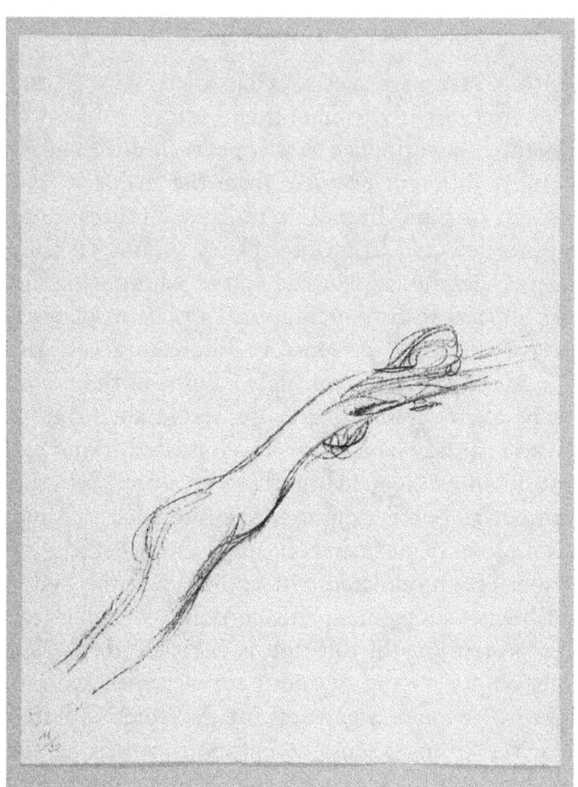

FIG. 2.1. Alberto Giacometti, 1960, lithographic pencil on transfer paper, 42 × 32.5 cm, published in *Paris sans fin* (1969), frontispiece.

Photo credit: Fondation Giacometti, Paris.

of vision as it is experienced. Drawing from what Clive Scott calls the 'in-textual reading' of a text, one could say that this visible rendering is a phenomenological translation of sight that, likewise, develops the view of the depicted from the 'inside'.[57] Such a 'constructivist' position begins with how a reader 'negotiates the act of reading itself' and engages with the text in a dynamic, open-ended way.[58] Mathews suggests that this open-endedness concerns the 'mobile and inevitable' translation of space and time into each other, which further provokes questions on 'the relation of art to thought, about the kind of thought in art'.[59] Merleau-Ponty's texture of vision can, in this sense, be seen as a translation of an interior perceiving into an exterior perceived via the stretching and spatializing of depiction as observed through the frontispiece figure.

In Giacometti's print we see this hinge of the interior and the exterior enacted through the line in its fluidity between trace and thread; it is at once the outline of a body and the weaving of surface, the movement of a stream and the mapping of space. This female nude thus plunges into the book as body and space, memory and texture. She gives the contour of visibility from vision, a visibility that depends on the line demarcating the interior from the exterior and vice versa. But the exterior, space, is white; the interior, the body, is empty. One is no longer sure where the body begins or where the space ends. The conjunction of the sensing and the sensed is invisible from the inside and the outside — the inside which is the outside, and vice versa — and the female nude stretches across with the light line of the crayon that enacts the imperfect line of history and sight, inside-out.

This lightness of the crayon is even more evident in plate 38 (see figure 2.2), which was created around 1964 and depicts Annette seated by the fireplace in their apartment on rue Mazarine (which they had bought in 1963).[60] In this print, the modulation of the density of the lines becomes quite evident, and in some places becomes so thin that it is barely visible. This refinement in lithography technique allowed Giacometti to create tonal contrasts in the lithographic line with the assistance of the highly-skilled printer Jean Célestin, and more importantly, to create illusions of erased lines which transfer lithography had ruled out due to its technical, material restrictions.[61]

The lines create planar perspective with the diagonal lines of the room corresponding to our focalization of Annette and her gaze upon the viewer. This perspective is, however, somewhat clouded due to the long near-horizontal lines that traverse the lower half of the print, almost obliterating or collapsing the foreground and the middle ground. Annette is embedded within a kind of middle space between the airy, porous nature of the foreground, and the more rigid planar structure of the background, and the viewer feels a sense of disequilibrium in looking at the print, both due to the unstable spatial construction of the room and the de-localized weight of the print.

While Annette takes up the highest and darkest concentration of lines within the print — which draws the attention of our gaze — other areas diffuse the weight and centrality of the print away from her. One such area is the small standing sculpture on the table to her left: not only does it seem to share our gaze in standing exactly

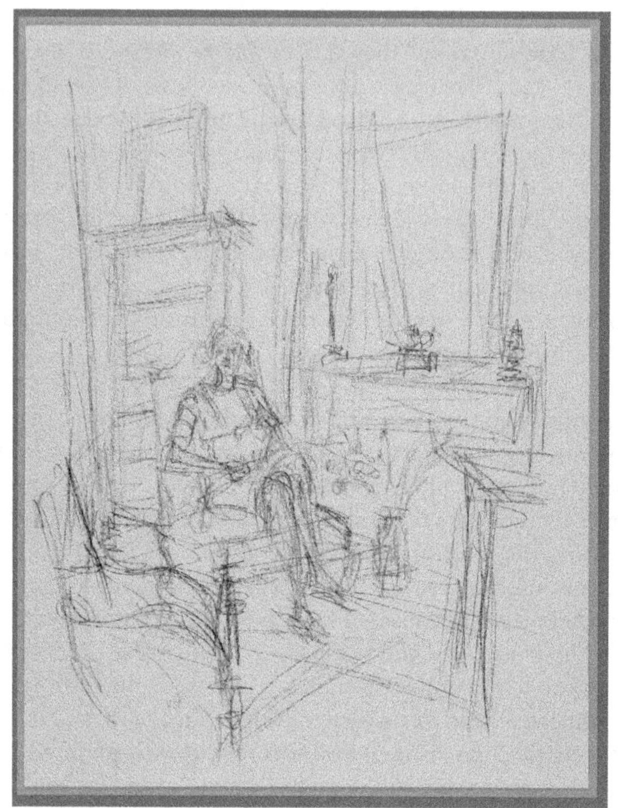

Fig. 2.2. Alberto Giacometti, 1964, lithographic pencil on transfer paper, 42 × 32.6 cm, published in *Paris sans fin* (1969), plate 38.

Photo credit: Fondation Giacometti, Paris.

at Annette's eye level, it is the object that gathers the tightest density of lines, almost like a clot, despite its size, thus setting it apart from the diffuse, porous and flimsy construction of its surrounding space. Next to this sculpture appears to be an opened window or mirror composed of swift downward lines broadly spaced. These rough, decisive marks detract from the focalization on Annette as a result of a shift in the weight of the crayon mark, but also due to the suggestion of a vague exterior space which gives the print a slit of possibility angled away from Annette.

Yet, if the viewer were to take a step back and look at the print from a greater distance, it would appear that Annette is tightly framed, or trapped, by four objects on each side: a ladder to the back, the window/mirror to her left, a structure that appears to extend from the desk to her front, and an armchair to her right. Therefore, there is an impression of a simultaneous compression of space and a partial collapse of depth in the print. This is largely due to a conflation of lines fulfilling different purposes. On the most fundamental level, there are traces depicting the shapes of objects (the armchair) and threads implying the texture of surfaces (the sculpture) or filling in for the plane of surfaces (the glass of the window or the image in the mirror). Yet at the same time we also have the diagonal and near-horizontal perspective lines that largely provide the direction of our gaze, but also obliterate it due to their repetition, overlapping and traversing objects and planes (this is most prominent for the long near-horizontal lines). Therefore, these lines are at counterpoint to each other not only in their composition of the print but also with our line of sight, thus creating a sense of disequilibrium in our looking at the print. The lightness of the crayon line becomes pivotal in constructing the lightness of space, which is experienced as both a tension and dissolution of depth and plane.

This can be seen all the more clearly when contrasted with Giacometti's earlier oil paintings, such as *The Artist's Mother* (1950), where our line of sight is clearly aligned with the planar construction and perspective of the painting, thus giving the viewer a sense of weighted and centralized space.[62] Here the planar construction of the room is emphasized by the repeated, overlapping lines which solidify the texture, thickness or materiality of the surfaces. This is in contrast to the lithograph print where many repeated lines actually cut across surfaces, obliterating or undercutting their three-dimensionality. One such significant area is that of the contact between Annette's lower body and the chair. The overlapping of repeated vertical, horizontal and diagonal lines compresses these surfaces together, giving the impression of surfaces bending and pressing against each other, thus creating an effect of flexibility in the boundaries of the planes which appear translucent, malleable and diffuse. Unlike the frontispiece of the nude figure, this illustration does not give the impression of a contour of flow or movement which constitutes space as body and vice-versa. Instead, the conflation of lines serving different purposes and overlapping one another results in a space wherein depth is constituted not through planar perspective, but through a temporal perspective of reading the print.

By this I mean that the contour of the line takes on the contour of memory, and specifically the layered, collapsible and diffused pathway of memory that remembering entails. In this print, we not only have traces that depict and threads that fill in, we also have rupture lines — such as those across Annette's legs, or the oblique diagonals in the upper left — that break through planes and surfaces (Ingold's third class). Being neither traces nor threads, these lines are not strictly visible or invisible. Rather, they take on Ingold's third class almost like rays of light or plumes of smoke that have the capacity to illuminate, occlude or obstruct our vision. In this sense they are not perspectival lines which direct our line of vision, but lines of perception which imply a direction of the sensory. The entire print, then, presents a woven texture that hovers between the visible and the non-visible in its trail of pathways of remembering. This is a texture that is not completely surface, for it still bears reminiscences of traces and threads, from which the viewer can pick out and work back through the processes of depiction, partially and visually.

This vague sense of incompletion presents a woven texture that seems to balance on the edge of the visible in taking us through the trails of constituting space as remembering space. The lithograph crayon in its pursuit of representing memory makes and weaves lines, eventually constituting a texture of the visible, but not quite — for the print returns to our gaze as a texture of unevenness and rupture, thread and trace, mark and light. In reading these lines, and the gaps in and between them, this texture takes on the line of remembering — of bringing to the fore an immanently faulty memory. In this sense, the line can only fail to collect and recollect space, but precisely in doing so, is able to enact the immanent loss of vision in memory and in the act of representing memory. Here again, the uncannily doubled and transferred erasures of the lithograph line return in their mortal guise.

Not Meant to Be Seen, nor Heard or Read?

In Giacometti's lithographs, then, lines (and the gaps between them) become entities that shape, modulate and generate a figure's spatiality and temporality from the surface of the prints, texts and blank pages. In Beckett's dramaticules, lines likewise take on such characteristics to translate and transform figures through narratives within and between theatre performances and dramatic texts. One crucial and fundamental aspect to this interaction is that the lines that are heard do not always correspond to the figures that are seen: a quick recollection of works such as *Not I*, *Footfalls* and *Rockaby* reveals a play of such distortion and coalescence.[63] In *Play* (1963) and *Come and Go* (1966) a third element becomes equally important: the lines that are read. These refer not just to the lines spoken by the characters but also to visual lines such as diagrams and stage representations.

This similar emphasis on the lines in the dramatic texts of *Play* and *Come and Go* may appear surprising given how differently these two plays are perceived in the theatre. *Play* presents three figures who are stuck in urns and forced to speak rapidly in 'toneless' voices whenever 'provoked by a spotlight projected on [their] faces alone',[64] whereas *Come and Go* presents three 'characters' sitting on a bench and exchanging very few words, the majority of which happen between two characters whenever a third exits the lit 'playing area'.[65] However, the element of the dramatic text enters both plays with the realization that not all lines that are spoken in the theatre — be they rapidly so in *Play* or inaudibly so in *Come and Go* — or read in the dramatic texts are meant to be heard by the viewer sitting in the audience. The issue of who or what provokes this 'meaning' derives from the impulse to interpret and narrativize when such lines of seeing, hearing and reading do not agree with each other.

For example, at the end of *Come and Go* a viewer observes the hands of the three women joined and clasped in such a way that each woman has contact with both others. A silence ensues before Flo says 'I can feel the rings' after which the play ends. What rings? Does the viewer take up what she or he sees ('no rings apparent') and unravel a possible line of narrative for why the rings have disappeared?[66] Or does the viewer believe what she or he hears, and either doubts what is seen ('no rings apparent') or projects metonymic and metaphoric lines of narratives from the kinds of rings that can still be felt? On the other hand, the reader who first reads the lines of the play will have every reason to believe that the rings are present on the hands: it is not until the next page that Beckett states, in a stage direction, that there are 'no rings apparent'.

The reader at this point has two further recourses to getting to the bottom of this ring issue: the stage diagram and the precise wording of the stage direction. Unlike the viewer in the theatre who only has a few seconds between the women's joining of hands and the falling of the curtains, the reader of the stage directions can ponder over the lines of the diagram long enough to understand how the hands are linked 'in the old way'.[67] Since Flo is the only one who has both Ru's and Vi's left hands, it seems to support the line of seeing in theatre to believe that those 'rings' refer to wedding rings — themselves images of linear connections between exteriority and interiority, as implied by the epigraph to this chapter — that are no longer there.[68] But scrutiny of the stage directions reveals that 'apparent' is a deliberate and difficult word because it begs the question: apparent to whom and in what way? All other items under the 'costume' heading in the stage directions were stated directly, such as 'light shoes with rubber soles' or 'drab nondescript hats', so why not state 'no rings worn' or simply 'no rings' to eliminate the puzzle?[69]

The word 'apparent' belongs to the same class of stage direction as the door and window of *Ghost Trio* which are left 'imperceptibly ajar'; such stage directions provoke questions of what or who creates such perceptions and to whom.[70] This provocation then generates a struggle of authority between three classes of lines. First, between the lines that are seen, heard and read; second, and by extension, the lines of narratives they generate and new ones which we fill in when there are gaps; third, and by implication, the lines of narration between focalization, voice and action. This struggle can be simplified to a question in relation to the above instance of *Come and Go*: who and where is the unreliable narrator here? If the narration of a written text is generally understood to consist of a voice (who speaks?) and a focalization (who sees?) — the combinations of which give rise to different degrees of knowledge shared with the reader through so-called unreliable narrators — then could this struggle be an enactment of the unreliability of such a narrator, without its appearance through textual or performed diegesis (for instance through a chorus as in Noh drama, or through a narrator-character in a memory play)?[71] In this light, *Come and Go* posits a narrator through the struggle of those three classes of lines; here we can draw an analogy with the doubled erasures that show up in Giacometti's lithographic line or to the six pages left and rendered blank.

This struggle between the three classes of lines that arise from interpreting between text and performance is made all the more pressing in perceiving the rapid lines of *Play*. The viewer struggles to make sense of these rapid, interrupted, criss-crossing lines during the course of the play, and this struggle is being made conscious upon the viewer's realization that the lines are being heard a second time in the play's repeat. This consciousness is doubled and questioned when the viewer realizes that this repeat does not allow them to hear any more clearly; and if these lines are not meant to be heard by way of narrative coherence and aural clarity, then why are they heard and in what other ways can one hear them?

A Truce and a Trace for a Space

This interrogation of wanting to hear or see, being conscious of not being able to do so and questioning the very nature of the needs that constitute such wants, that perhaps one's belief of needing had in the first place been misguided, can be traced back to Beckett's aesthetic writings of the 1930s. In his essay 'Les Deux Besoins' [The Two Needs] written in 1938, Beckett represents the difficult condition of seeing as a consequence of the chaos of wanting to see ('issue du chaos de vouloir voir') and entering into the nothingness of having seen ('entrée dans le néant d'avoir vu').[72] This condition, crucially, is one that he represented spatially and temporally (from axis Aab to Dde in a diagram Beckett provided) within the larger dodecahedronal matrix of a creative autology ('l'autologie créatrice').[73]

Beckett explains the composition of this matrix in the following way:

> Besoin d'avoir besoin (DEF) et besoin dont on a besoin (ABC), conscience du besoin d'avoir besoin (ab) et conscience du besoin dont on a besoin — dont on *avait* besoin (de), issue du chaos de vouloir voir (Aab) et entrée dans le néant d'avoir vu (Dde), déclenchement et fin de l'autologie créatrice (abcdef). Voilà par exemple une façon comme une autre d'indiquer les limites entre lesquelles l'artiste se met à la question, se met en question, se résout en questions, en questions rhétoriques sans function oratoire.[74]
>
> [Need to need (DEF) and the need of which one has need (ABC), awareness of the need to need (ab) and awareness of the need of which one has need — of which was needed (de), results from the chaos of wanting to see (Aab) and enters into the nothingness of having seen (Dde), triggering and ending the creative autology (abcdef). Here is an example of a way, like any other, of indicating the limits between which an artist confronts the question, is put into question, turns to questions, in rhetorical questions without oratory function.]

It is very difficult to see one's way through this highly complex piece of writing in the very ways that the lines of text, diagram and meaning intersect. Such a need to synthesize and decipher from these lines a coherent line of meaning is perhaps itself made reflexive by the content of this writing; yet one must try. According to this matrix, the very source and end of seeing lies in the dual nature of what one believes one needs and what one has need of; this incompatibility between the desired and the necessitated need results in the condition of 'wanting to see' spiralling into the condition of 'having seen nothing'. Such concerns can also be seen in 'Intercessions by Dennis Devlin' written in the same year, in which Beckett describes this 'inverted spiral of need' as one that 'condenses in intensity and brightness from the mere need of the angels to that of the seraphinns [*sic*], whose end is its own end in the end and the source of need'.[75] The relationship between the desire to see and the result of seeing nothing is thus inextricable from the relation between the realization of one's need to see and the realization of the very nature of this realization. This relationship is one that is consequent, temporal, spatial and circular.

In fact, in many of Beckett's writings, such an interrogation of wanting to see, being conscious of not being able to do so, and questioning the very nature of the needs that constitute such wants, is framed in terms of seeing through words and associated with surface, rupture and trace — the very terminologies of Ingold's anthropological framework of the line. In his letter in German written to Axel Kaun, Beckett mentions the need to tear apart the 'veil' of language to get at the things or the nothingness behind it, and further restates this a few lines down as the need to 'bore one hole after another' in language, 'until what lurks behind it — be it something or nothing — begins to seep through'.[76] This pursuit or retrieval of the hidden or secretive 'something' or 'nothing' behind language is also evident in his writing on poetry and visual art. In his description of the language at work in Devlin's poetry, he writes of the 'insistence with which the ground invades the surface' throughout the poem, and how certain passages which on 'fourth or fifth reading seemed to sag' would 'tighten into line' — a play on tightening in terms of 'falling into line' after misbehaving, or analogously to material lines that only work if they are tight, like washing lines or tightropes.[77] In 'Pour Avigdor Arikha' which Beckett wrote for an exhibition of the artist's drawings in 1966, this interrogation of the 'something' or 'nothing' behind is once again linked to the struggle to see, but also the struggle to make:

> Siège remis devant le dehors imprenable. Fièvre œil-main dans la soif du non-soi. Œil par la main sans cesse changé à l'instant même où sans cesse il la change. Regard ne s'arrachant à l'invisible que pour s'asséner sur l'infaisable et retour éclair. Trêve à la navette et traces de ce que c'est que d'être et d'être devant. Traces profondes.
>
> [Siege laid again to the impregnable without. Eye and hand fevering after the unself. By the hand it unceasingly changes the eye unceasingly changed. Back and forth the gaze beating against unseeable and unmakable. Truce for a space and the marks of what it is to be and be in face of. Those deep marks to show.][78]

'Trêve' is here contrasted with 'trace' and yet contains also *rêve*; where 'trêve' comes into place, 'trace' finds an emerging. This revealing of the mark is characterized by the difficulty of seeing and making between 'l'invisible' and 'l'infaisable', 'unseeable' and 'unmakable', but these marks 'show'; the struggling founded on the difficulty in seeing and making nevertheless gives that position of 'trêve' and 'trace'.

Narration, or more precisely the potential to narrate, as the blank space of possibility could be seen to occupy such a position in the two dramaticules, but their use of light and silence offers another reading. In *Play*, the lines of the three characters are 'provoked by a spotlight projected on faces alone' and spoken with 'toneless' voices and at 'rapid tempo'; this beam of light swings rapidly from a 'single' spot that 'must not be situated outside the ideal space (stage) occupied by its victims', and like a 'unique inquisitor' must 'swivel' at 'maximum speed from one face to another'.[79] The dramatic text makes overt that light is a type of character in its own right, which the performed light further emphasizes by giving the effect of its making words from speech. Due to the extreme rapidity with which the lines are delivered and further interrupted by the lines of the preceding or following characters, the audience is only able to pick up certain words or phrases that are repeated or intercepted. Here is one such instance:

> W2 What do you do when you go out? Sift?
> [*Spot from W2 to M.*]
> M Am I hiding something? *Have I lost* —
> [*Spot from M to W1.*]
> W1 She had means, I fancy, though she lived like a pig.
> [*Spot from W1 to W2.*]
> W2 Like dragging a great roller, on a scorching day. The strain... to get it moving, momentum coming —
> [*Spot off W2. Blackout. Three seconds. Spot on W2.*]
> W2 Kill it and strain again.
> [*Spot from W2 to M.*]
> M *Have I lost*... the thing you want? Why go out? *Why go* —
> [*Spot from M to W2.*]
> W2 And you perhaps pitying me, thinking, Poor thing, she needs a rest.
> [*Spot from W2 to W1.*]
> W1 Perhaps she has taken him away to live... somewhere in the sun.
> [*Spot from W1 to M.*]
> M *Why go* down? *Why not* —
> [*Spot from M to W2.*]
> W2 I don't know.
> [*Spot from W2 to W1.*]
> W1 Perhaps she is sitting somewhere, by the open window, her hands folded in her lap, gazing down out over the olives —
> [*Spot from W1 to M.*]
> M *Why not* keep on glaring at me without ceasing? I might start to rave and — [*Hiccup*] — bring it up for you. *Par-*
> [*Spot from M to W2.*]
> W2 No.
> [*Spot from W2 to M.*]
> M *-don.*[80]

The words which would stand out the most in performance are those of M which are intercepted (emphasized with italics above) and the single line of W2 uttered after the respite of the blackout. In both cases, it is the spoken line that has been broken, interrupted or disjointed by the line of light that enables words to be heard. The weaving of the word from the line of speech to the line of hearing is incomplete and fractured, but it is precisely by way of this rupture that these stitches of the thread, its 'profound traces' ('traces profondes'), show up briefly and are heard before the line is again tightened as ceaseless, monotonous and rapid speech.

By contrast, in *Come and Go*, the disjunction between the lines that are heard and the lines that are spoken shows up in the silence that intercepts speech, rather than in speech intercepted by silence as observed above in *Play*:

> RU On the log.
> [*Silence.*
> Exit *Flo* left.
> *Silence.*]
> Vi.
> VI Yes.
> RU How do you find Flo?
> VI She seems much the same. [Ru *moves to centre seat, whispers in* Vi's *ear. Appalled.*] Oh! [*They look at each other.* Ru *puts her finger to her lips.*] Has she not been told?
> RU God forbid.[81]

Unlike in *Play*, the audience of *Come and Go* is able to pick up with utter clarity all the lines that are heard in the theatre, but like *Play*, not all lines that are spoken in *Come and Go* are meant to be heard. The inaudible lines that are whispered between the characters generate the geometrical pyramid of our need to hear more clearly, and the lines that are silenced between every pair of characters with a finger to the lips gestures to the impossibility of our ever hearing. Here then, a movement from the chaos of wanting to hear to the nothingness of having heard; each character, like the audience, has her turn at not being able to hear what in the first place was not capable of being heard. Therefore, the lines that are not meant to be heard are conflated with the lines that are not spoken — here the space and mark of *trêve* and *trace* coalesce into a doubled erasure.

Displaced Sight

This lack of translation between spoken and audible lines is further intensified by the conflation of the characters' need to see and be seen with the audience's need to see and the nothingness of having seen. In both plays, the characters speak of not being seen or not being able to see: M utters 'Am I as much as... being seen?' three times in *Play*, while Flo says that 'one sees little in this light' in *Come and Go*.[82] The audience, likewise, is obstructed in their line of vision due to light: in *Play* the audience is only allowed to see what the line of light illuminates at any single moment, whereas in *Come and Go* Beckett specifies that it 'should not be clear what they are sitting on' and that they 'are not seen to go off stage' during the play.[83]

The difficulty in seeing is perpetuated over the space and duration of staged visual images and figure movements which remain largely repetitive and static. In *Play* the ceaseless transfer of rapid spoken lines is delivered from static bodies hosted in three linear structures (urns), whereas in *Come and Go* the secrets that we are not allowed to hear and are unable to see are staged with immaculately choreographed movements and positions that are slow, symmetrical and deliberate. Both plays involve structural repeats: in *Play* the entire play is repeated once, with a third attempt indicated at the close of the play, whereas in *Come and Go* each woman leaves the stage once, resulting in three near-identical episodes of the remaining pair of women sharing a secret about the one who is absent. The experience of the audience is one in which the spoken lines of the figures are increasingly detached from the staged visual image that remains static and left behind; the sense of disequilibrium is a result of our line of hearing being at a disjuncture with our line of sight.

The stage becomes the ceaseless space and duration of the fall from the chaos of wanting to see/hear to the nothingness of having seen/heard; the figures become the site of enactment for the linear trajectory of Beckett's 'Les Deux Besoins'. But this trajectory finds its origins and its end in the very circulation of the space. In the two works where spoken lines seem to diverge from those heard and seen, the figures that remain are figures of displacement. In 'L'Oscillation distinct' [Distinct Oscillation], Jean-Luc Nancy differentiates such displacement from emptiness. As the 'empty place of the absent as a place that is not empty', displacement is a diegesis of emptiness that gives the possibility of narration in space:

> The word *imago* designated the effigy of the absent, the dead, and, more precisely, the ancestors: the dead from whom we come, the links of the lineage in which each of us is a stitch. [...] The absent are not there, are not 'in images'. But they are imaged: their absence is woven into our presence. The empty place of the absent as a place that is not empty: that is the image. A place that is not empty does not mean a place that has been filled: it means the place of the image, that is, in the end, the image as place, and a singular place for what has no place here: the place of a displacement, a metaphor — and here we are again.[84]

The figures in these two dramaticules can, therefore, be seen as figures of displacement that weave the absent and the present into multiple textiles of reading. In both of these plays, the rift between the spoken lines, audible lines and visual lines generates accumulating tension between our need to see/hear and our impossibility to do so, further exacerbated by the characters' abilities and inabilities to do the same. As the plays are dragged out in a process of repetition, our line of hearing is stretched further away from our line of seeing due to the disjuncture between the continuous and the static. Yet at the same time, the circularity of the lines that are heard gives the impression of the line of the story retracing its own steps, therefore dissolving the linearity of time and giving the impression of aural figuration re-joining static visualized figures as traces of memory. The figure becomes a space of displacement and replacement. It is this process of achieving the staged image that perhaps comes close to enacting what Beckett insistently refers to as the boring of holes within the surface of the language.

In these two plays and Giacometti's lithographs, it is the linear structure of the figures and their figurations that enable the transferring and transforming of senses, spaces and narratives. These processes stage ways of performing visibility in spite of recursive invisibility. In the residual figuration of a figure as displacement, we find a truce — a 'something' as much as a 'nothing' — which, even though is merely a temporary ceasefire, enacts the narrativity of possibility.

Notes to Chapter 2

1. Aulus Gellius, *Attic Nights*, II, 237.
2. Samuel Beckett, *Rockaby*, in *The Complete Dramatic Works*, pp. 431–42 (p. 442).
3. Tim Ingold, *Lines: A Brief History* (London: Routledge, 2016). Maurice Merleau-Ponty, 'Eye and Mind', in *The Merleau-Ponty Aesthetics Reader: Philosophy and Painting*, ed. by Galen A. Johnson (Evanston, IL: Northwestern University Press, 1993), pp. 121–49.
4. Ingold, *Lines*, p. 42.
5. Elizabeth Wayland Barber, *Women's Work: The First 20,000 Years. Women, Cloth, and Society in Early Times* (New York: W. W. Norton, 1994), p. 45. David Turnbull, 'String and Stories', in *Encyclopaedia of the History of Science, Technology, and Medicine in Non-western Cultures*, ed. by Helaine Selin (Berlin: Springer, 2008), pp. 2042–44 (p. 2043).
6. Samuel Beckett, *Watt* (London: Faber & Faber, 2009), pp. 23–24. For more on Watt's walking, see Steven Connor, 'Auf Schwankendem Boden', in *Samuel Beckett, Bruce Nauman* (Vienna: Kunsthalle Wien, 2000), pp. 80–87. Translated as 'Shifting Ground' <www. stevenconnor.com/ beckettnauman/> [accessed 6 July 2021].
7. Samuel Beckett, *...but the clouds...*, in *The Complete Dramatic Works*, pp. 415–22 (p. 419).
8. For comparative studies of the walker and walking in the works of Beckett and Giacometti, see Mathews, 'Walking with Angels in Giacometti and Beckett'; James Olney, *Memory and Narrative: The Weave of Life-writing* (Chicago, IL: University of Chicago Press, 1998); Jeffrey Cane Robinson, *The Walk: Notes on a Romantic Image* (Rochester: Dalkey Archive Press, 2006).
9. Samuel Beckett, *Footfalls*, in *The Complete Dramatic Works*, pp. 397–404 (p. 399).
10. Ibid., pp. 401, 402.
11. Ibid., pp. 402–03.
12. Anna McMullan, 'Samuel Beckett's Scenographic Collaboration with Jocelyn Herbert', *Degrés: revue de synthèse à orientation sémiologique*, 149 (2012), 1–17 (p. 16).
13. Beckett, *Footfalls*, in *The Complete Dramatic Works*, pp. 397–403 (p. 399).
14. Gidal, *Understanding Beckett*, p. 163.For more on *Footfalls* and steps, see Enoch Brater, 'A Footnote to *Footfalls*: Footsteps of Infinity on Beckett's Narrow Space', *Comparative Drama*, 12 (1978), 35–41; R. Thomas Simone, '"Faint, Though by No Means Invisible": A Commentary on Beckett's *Footfalls*', *Modern Drama*, 26 (1983), 435–46.
15. Ingold, *Lines*, p. 44.
16. Ibid., p. 45.
17. Ibid., p. 46.
18. Ibid.
19. The connections between 'text' and 'textile' are abundant in literary scholarship; for example, see 'basting' in Jacques Derrida, *Writing and Difference*, trans. by Alan Bass (Chicago, IL: University of Chicago Press, 1978), p. xiv, and 'hyphology' in Roland Barthes, *The Pleasure of the Text*, trans. by Richard Miller (New York: Hill & Wang, 1975), p. 64.
20. This work, *Seated Women and Men's Heads* (1962), can be viewed at the Alberto Giacometti Database (AGD 936) <https://www.fondation-giacometti.fr/en/database/173157/seated-women-and-mens-heads> [accessed 6 July 2021].
21. Ingold, *Lines*, pp. 49–50.
22. Ibid., pp. 50–51.
23. See *Act Without Words II*, *Film*, *Come and Go*, *Footfalls*, *Ghost Trio*, *...but the clouds...*, *Quad* and *What Where*. *Play* has not so much a diagram as a score for the chorus of voices.

24. See Fehsenfeld, '"Everything Out But the Faces"'.
25. See Samuel Beckett and Alan Schneider, *No Author Better Served: The Correspondence of Samuel Beckett & Alan Schneider*, ed. by Maurice Harmon (Cambridge, MA: Harvard University Press, 1998), pp. 416, 22.
26. Samuel Beckett, *Quad*, in *The Complete Dramatic Works*, pp. 449–54 (p. 451). For geometry and arithmetic in *Quad* and in Beckett more generally, see Chris Ackerley, '"Ever Know What Happened?"': Shades and Echoes in Samuel Beckett's Television Plays', *Journal of Beckett Studies*, 18 (2009), 136–64; Brett Stevens, 'A Purgatorial Calculus: Beckett's Mathematics in *Quad*', in *A Companion to Samuel Beckett*, ed. by Stanley E. Gontarski (Oxford: Blackwell, 2010), pp. 164–81; Chris Ackerley, 'Samuel Beckett: The Geometry of the Imagination', in *Samuel Beckett: Debts and Legacies. New Critical Essays*, ed. by Peter Fifield and David Addyman (London: Bloomsbury, 2013), pp. 85–108.
27. Beckett, *Quad*, p. 453.
28. Merleau-Ponty, 'Eye and Mind', p. 125.
29. For an overview of Merleau-Ponty and Sartre on doubt in the two artists, see Theodore Toadvine, 'The Art of Doubting: Merleau-Ponty and Cézanne', *Philosophy Today*, 41.4 (1997), 545–53.
30. Merleau-Ponty, 'Eye and Mind', p. 124.
31. Ibid., p. 125.
32. Ibid., p. 132. For Merleau-Ponty's full-fledged exposition on the chiasm, see Maurice Merleau-Ponty, 'The Intertwining — The Chiasm', in *The Visible and the Invisible*, ed. by Claude Lefort, trans. by Alberto Lingis (Evanston, IL: Northwestern University Press, 1968), pp. 130–55.
33. Merleau-Ponty, 'Eye and Mind', p. 140.
34. Ibid., p. 143.
35. Ibid.
36. Ibid., p. 144.
37. Ibid.
38. Ibid., pp. 144, 143.
39. Glen A. Mazis, 'Merleau-Ponty's Artist of Depth: Exploring "Eye and Mind" and the Works of Art Chosen by Merleau-Ponty as Preface', *PhaenEx*, 7 (2012), 244–74 (pp. 265–66).
40. Brendan Prendeville, 'Merleau-Ponty, Realism and Painting: Psychophysical Space and the Space of Exchange', *Art History*, 22 (1999), 364–88 (p. 377).
41. Merleau-Ponty, 'Eye and Mind', p. 144.
42. Sylvie Wuhrmann, 'Paris sans fin ou la libération du regard', in Alberto Giacometti, *Paris sans fin* (Paris: Buchet & Chastel, 2003), pp. 7–20 (p. 11).
43. See Véronique Wiesinger, *Giacometti Without End* (Hong Kong: Gagosian Gallery, 2014), p. 21.
44. Ibid., p. 151.
45. 'Quinze, non, seize mai 1964, dans ma chambre [...] j'ai essayé de reprendre, vues des rues, intérieurs, cela ne va plus, où, comment reprendre?' (Giacometti, *Paris sans fin*, n.p.).
46. See Ingold, *Lines*, p. 83.
47. For the graphic in writing and reading, see Scott, *Literary Translation and the Rediscovery of Reading*, and *Translating the Perception of Text : Literary Translation and Phenomenology*.
48. For narrativity and narration in visual art, see for example Ernst van Alphen, 'The Narrative of Perception and the Perception of Narrative', and *Francis Bacon and the Loss of Self* (London: Reaktion books, 1992).
49. For *Paris sans fin* and its cinematic organization, see Herbert C. Lust, *Giacometti: The Complete Graphics and 15 Drawings* (New York: Tudor, 1970).
50. Giacometti, *Paris sans fin*, n.p. All translations are my own unless stated otherwise.
51. Wiesinger, *Giacometti Without End*, p. 161.
52. Wuhrmann, 'Paris sans fin ou la libération du regard', p. 16.
53. Wiesinger, *Giacometti Without End*, p. 69.
54. Ibid.
55. Ibid.
56. Merleau-Ponty, 'Eye and Mind', p. 126.

57. Scott, *Literary Translation and the Rediscovery of Reading*, p. 2.
58. Ibid., p. 14.
59. Mathews, *Alberto Giacometti*, p. 123.
60. Wiesinger, *Giacometti Without End*, p. 105.
61. Ibid., p. 69.
62. This work can be viewed at the MoMA website <https://www.moma.org/collection/works/78448> [accessed 6 July 2021].
63. For the centrality of this phenomenon in Beckett's dramaticules, see for example Enoch Brater, *Beyond Minimalism: Beckett's Late Style in the Theater* (Oxford: Oxford University Press, 1990); Anna McMullan, *Theatre on Trial: Samuel Beckett's Later Drama* (London: Routledge, 2003); Jeanette R. Malkin, *Memory-theater and Postmodern Drama* (Ann Arbor: University of Michigan Press, 1999).
64. Beckett, *Play*, p. 307.
65. Samuel Beckett, *Come and Go*, in *The Complete Dramatic Works*, pp. 351–58 (pp. 353, 356).
66. Ibid., pp. 355, 356.
67. Ibid., p. 355.
68. See Keir Elam, 'Dead Heads: Damnation-narration in the "Dramaticules"', in *The Cambridge Companion to Beckett*, ed. by Pilling, pp. 145–66; Hersch Zeifman, 'Come and Go: A Criticule', in *Samuel Beckett: Humanistic Perspectives*, ed. by M. Beja, S. E. Gontarski, and P. Astier (Columbus: Ohio State University Press, 1983), pp. 137–44; Karen Laughlin, '"Looking for Sense...": The Spectator's Response to Beckett's Come and Go', *Modern Drama*, 30 (1987), 137–46.
69. Beckett, *Come and Go*, p. 356.
70. Samuel Beckett, *Ghost Trio*, in *The Complete Dramatic Works*, pp. 405–14 (p. 408).
71. I take, for now, Genette's formulation in *Narrative Discourse*, originally published in French in 1972 as *Figures III*. This formulation and other alternatives will be discussed in detail in the next chapter. See Gérard Genette, *Narrative Discourse: An Essay in Method*, trans. by Jane E. Lewin (Ithaca, NY: Cornell University Press, 1983).
72. Samuel Beckett, , 'Les Deux Besoins', in *Disjecta: Miscellaneous Writings and a Dramatic Fragment* (London: Calder, 1983), pp. 55–57 (p. 56).
73. Ibid.
74. Ibid.
75. Samuel Beckett, 'Intercessions by Dennis Devlin', in *Disjecta*, pp. 91–94 (p. 92).
76. Beckett, *Disjecta*, p. 172. The original German is: 'Und immer mehr wie ein Schleier kommt mir meine Sprache vor, den man zerreissen muss, um an die dahinterliegenden Dinge (oder das dahinterliegende Nichts) zu kommen. [...] Ein Loch nach dem andern in ihr zu bohren, bis das Dahinterkauernde, sei es etwas oder nichts, durchzusickern anfängt' (ibid., p. 52).
77. Beckett, 'Intercessions by Dennis Devlin', p. 94.
78. Samuel Beckett, 'Pour Avigdor Arikha', in *Disjecta*, p. 152. Translation by Beckett in 1967 for Arikha's exhibitions in England and the States.
79. Beckett, *Play*, pp. 307, 318.
80. Ibid., pp. 315–16 (my emphasis).
81. Beckett, *Come and Go*, p. 354.
82. Beckett, *Play*, p. 317; *Come and Go*, p. 355.
83. Beckett, *Come and Go*, p. 356.
84. Jean-Luc Nancy, 'Distinct Oscillation', in *The Ground of the Image*, trans. by Jeff Fort (New York: Fordham University Press, 2005), pp. 63–79 (pp. 67–68).

CHAPTER 3

Hollow Focalizations in *All That Fall*, *Embers* and the Diego Paintings

> I have read in our annals that at the time when the army of the Roman people was cut to pieces at Cannae, an aged mother was overwhelmed with grief and sorrow by a message announcing the death of her son; but that report was false, and when not long afterwards the young man returned from that battle to the city, the aged mother, upon suddenly seeing her son, was overpowered by the flood, the shock, and the crash, so to speak, of unlooked-for joy descending upon her, and gave up the ghost.
>
> — Aulus Gellius, *Attic Nights*, Book 3[1]

The previous two chapters have explored spatial depictions and perceptions of figures in different ways. Chapter 1 looked at how distance is created and perceived between the space of the figure and the space of the viewer through scale and frame, and Chapter 2 explored how the dramatic and textual spaces of the dramaticules and lithographs are broken down through lines and linear forms that transfer and translate narratives and senses. These interrogations of spatial positioning bring with them a whole host of implications for the way a figure is placed in multiple frames of time and narrative. A late Giacometti bust, for instance, can be understood in markedly different ways when displayed as part of a series of similar-looking busts whose production narrative cannot be recovered, or when seen from the distance from which Giacometti had sculpted the model — a distance that recovers a semblance of looking at, or displays a reflection of our looking closely, or uncovers that distance as merely one version of looking amidst Giacometti's countless revisions made from memory. In these analyses, the spectral dimension of the figure creeps up when aspects of its production are superimposed with those of erasure. The figuration enters the figure and vice versa, thus rendering the notion of figure necessarily incomplete and residual. However, this ghostly figure is characterized differently in radio drama and Giacometti's painted portraits: it is immediately apparent in its depiction, and forcefully so through the superimposition of theatrical diegesis and visual deictic traces. This depictive move can be framed in terms of focalization, and it is this focalization rendered multiply mobile that allows the ghostly figure to rear its head from the start, in turn producing unexpected effects of residual figuration.

Focalization is a complex starting point with which to begin any textual analysis, let alone a comparative analysis of verbal and visual works of different media. This is because the term is used both in the literary and visual domains, and it has come to mean very different things in the hands of different scholars coming after Gérard Genette and his formulation of the term in *Narrative Discourse.*[2] In Genette's typology, focalization in a narrative can be aligned with the question of 'who sees?', and must be distinguished from voice, which is aligned with the question 'who speaks?'; in this respect focalization thus avoids the confusion between sight and speech in discussions of narrative 'point of view'.[3] Genette describes three levels of focalization according to how much a narrator says in comparison to what a character knows: zero focalization (typically aligned with an omniscient narrator) where a narrator '*says* more than any of the characters knows', internal focalization where the narrator 'says only what a given character knows', and thus implies a 'restriction of field', and external focalization where the narrator 'says less than the character knows'.[4]

Focalization thus seems to be a very useful point of entry to reading Beckett's radio plays and Giacometti's painted portraits, because these works complicate figure and space primarily by interrogating a figure's position(s) of looking or speaking in relation to other elements of the work. These questions can be broadly formulated to 'from where does the figure speak?' and 'from where does the figure look?'. For instance, such questions might arise when a listener of *Embers* first hears Ada's voice: she advises Henry not to sit on 'the cold stones' and to allow her to 'slip [her] shawl under', which implies that she is speaking from the same place as Henry; yet according to the stage directions, she makes 'no sound as she sits', which suggests that her voice comes from a body that does not exist in the same visible space as Henry's, which by means of sound effects, does appear to produce noise.[5] Sometimes the difficulty in positioning the figure derives not only from the relation between his or her speaking and other characters, but also from the relation between the speaking and the positions within the figure's body from which the words could have originated. In other words, the figure could be speaking to him or herself in the mind without having the words depart from his or her mouth, hence the listener finds him or herself quite suddenly placed into the figure's mind, to which no other characters in the play have access. Such ways of swiftly and invisibly manipulating what the listener sees and hears in relation to the different types of voices generated by words thus make it possible to create various degrees of spectral figures. Genette's typology of focalization and voice becomes a useful framework to begin analysing this play of sight and sound in relation to narrators and narratives in radio drama.[6]

In *Travelling Concepts in the Humanities*, Mieke Bal outlines a further development of focalization that is particularly useful for a comparative reading of radio plays and paintings.[7] First, her focalization is a term that has travelled from the visual domain ('focusing with a lens'), to narratology ('the cluster of perception and interpretation that guides the attention through the narrative'), and then to visual analysis, where it has attained a different meaning that 'indicates neither a *location* of the gaze on the picture plane, nor a *subject* of it, such as either the figure or the viewer'; instead, 'what becomes visible is the *movement* of the look'.[8] This means that focalization, for Bal, specifies the 'relation between the seeing subject and the object seen' rather than 'a simple distribution of information within the text'.[9] On this count, Bal importantly diverges from Genette, because every focalization entails a relation of subjectivity, and therefore there can be no neutral or unfocalized narrative for her. Second, this relation of subjectivity is crucially linked to deixis via Émile Benveniste, whose work has already been mentioned in the Introduction in relation to Bryson's notion of the deictic trace in visual art.[10] For both Bryson and Bal, Benveniste's formulation is original because it posits that reference is secondary to deixis, which is the 'I-you' interaction that constitutes a 'referential merry-go-round'; this interaction produces subjectivity in language and undermines the 'subject/object opposition promoted by reference' and, by implication, 'individual authority' in its various forms across cultural texts.[11] Third, such an understanding of subjectivity in focalization thus places the focus of interpretation on structures of framing that shape the constant changes of the 'I-you' exchange, rather than on meaning to be found in the 'product of reference' or in 'authorial intention'. Such a framework of focalization is thus able to incorporate the ambiguity of the gaze as understood between the Lacanian gaze and its more ordinary use which is 'synonymous with the Lacanian look'. It is by means of the negotiation of her or his position within this ambiguity that the 'unstable holder of the look' produces focalization in the mobility of the 'I' and 'you'.[12]

This emphasis on the movement and mobility of focalization in relation to structures of framing that shape and make figures seems highly relevant to a comparative reading of Beckett's radio plays and Giacometti's portrait paintings. For instance, most of Giacometti's portrait paintings incorporate multiple levels of framing that serve both to situate the position of the depicted figure within a centralized mimetic space and to direct our looking at the painting which has been rendered flat by the deictic marks of roughly painted frames within material ones. The figure becomes the locus of the subject of depiction and the object of perception, the looking and the looked. This is closely analogous, for instance, to moments in *All That Fall* when the listener realizes that the words Maddy speaks are no longer heard by the people around her; by being moved into her mind, the listener looks through Maddy as the subject of speaking, rather than at her in the position of the recipient of her spoken words together with the other characters in the play.

In both cases, the mobility of the focalization appears to be a result of creating figures, or their impressions, by changing their relation to grounds. As observed by Steven Connor, 'It is in radio that Beckett seems to have found the possibility of writing without ground — that is to say, writing in which the spoken words are at once figure and ground'.[13] In order to understand how figure-ground relations shape focalizations in radio plays and paintings, one can begin by examining broad conceptualizations of how spatial relations feature in discussions about figure and ground. Such a survey will then inform analyses of how grounds of meaning in

All That Fall, *Embers* and the Diego paintings appear to shift constantly beneath the figures, which results in focalizations characterized by acts of excavating and hollowed-out figures.

Focalization Between Figure and Ground

> Their farewell was memorable. Neary came out of one of his dead sleeps and said:
> 'Murphy, all life is figure and ground'.
> 'But a wandering to find home,' said Murphy.
> 'The face,' said Neary, 'or system of faces, against the big blooming buzzing confusion. I think of Miss Dwyer'.
>
> — SAMUEL BECKETT, *Murphy*

> The baby, assailed by eyes, ears, nose, skin, and entrails at once, feels it all as one great blooming, buzzing confusion; and to the very end of life, our location of all things in one space is due to the fact that the original extents or bignesses of all the sensations which came to our notice at once, coalesced together into one and the same space.
>
> — WILLIAM JAMES, *The Principles of Psychology*[14]

In his brief quotation of William James, Neary draws our attention to the overarching relationship between figure and ground with the preposition 'against': it is not only that the baby is assailed by this corporeal confusion all at once temporally and spatially, he or she is drawn to faces in this ground, and singles out particular faces as figures against this vague ground. Taking this as the basic prepositional relation between figure and ground, the three figure-ground approaches that James Elkins proposes in his book *On Pictures and the Words That Fail Them* can be understood as a development of this 'against' into a gradation of 'between', 'within' and 'into'.

The first approach, the relation 'between', is structural as it demarcates figure and ground through analyses of formal elements of composition such as line, point and shape. This can be seen in the works of the Danish experimental psychologist Edgar Rubin, and the 1940s Gestalt psychologists Walter Ehrenstein and Kurt Goldstein. Belonging to the second approach, the relation 'within', are psychological and psychoanalytic interpretations which prioritize the phenomenological situating of figure within ground and the conscious and unconscious thought processes that give rise to that. To illustrate this, Elkins turns towards Merleau-Ponty, Deleuze and the modernism scholar Rosalind Krauss, whose figure-ground framework he critiques mainly through Lacan and Lyotard. The third approach, the relation 'into', emphasizes movement and process: the inflection and circulation of figure into ground, and vice versa, become the main characteristics of the constantly changing figure-ground relationship. This approach, Elkins argues, is best characterized as psychology informed by its 'conceptual roots in the Aristotelian concepts of change, matter, and form'.[15]

These categories open up ways of thinking about how spatial relations between figure and ground are intricately bound to movements not only in perception, but also in time, narrative and memory. Such an understanding, no doubt, allows a productive basis of comparing focalization in works across different media. In fact, it is such an understanding that shows how approaches belonging to different groups in Elkins's categorization actually find reverberations in each other. A juxtaposition of Rubin's vase (belonging to Elkins's first group) and Krauss's Klein group (Elkins's second group) would exemplify such a case in point.[16]

In 'Figure and Ground', Rubin established various formal aspects that distinguish figure from ground, namely shape, subject-character, colour, distance, memory and emotions. What a viewer considers as ground in contrast to a figure is usually characterized as being shapeless, lacking in subject-character, less prominent in colour and positioned further away from the figure. Because of these attributes, the ground is forgettable and is not retained in our memory. When a figure and its ground share the same contours such as in Rubin's vase, the ground can become the figure with a shift in perception: this happens when it comes to the fore as a shaped thing and ceases to be a neutral, unobtrusive plane. Concentrating on the background against which a viewer sees the vase would now bring up two facial silhouettes instead: the ground-now-figure thus captures our attention and remains in our memory for a longer. In other words, the ground, in becoming figure, shifts from a there and then to a here and now. This spatio-temporal shift in perception bears upon the ambiguity of the shared contour between figure and ground. The experience of the image can be likened to the coalescence of sensations in William James's 'one and the same space' wherein the whole is dependent on — and yet exceeds the sum of — its parts.

This formal binary between figure and ground would be turned inside-out by Rosalind Krauss in *The Optical Unconscious* almost eighty years later. She posits a structuralist Klein group to demarcate the polarities, or what she calls the 'logic of the double negative', of figure and ground in modernist art. The group — which is related to the Greimas square and also employed by Jameson and Claude Lévi-Strauss — is a four-fold field of mirror inversion wherein figure and ground are posed in opposition not only to each other, but also to not-figure and not-ground simultaneously. The Klein group re-orders the possibilities of the binary opposition between figure and ground against its negatives, pitting the upper 'complex' axis of figure/ground against its 'shadow correlates' — characterized by the space of the flexible 'maybe' — of the 'neutral' axis of not-figure/ not-ground.[17]

Krauss's Klein group orders the ambiguity of Rubin's spatio-temporal shift into a circulation of multiply negated axes and plots these against themselves. Such a diagram, according to Krauss, expresses both the energy of modernism and its 'complete self-enclosure' through its unfolding eight vertices.[18] How precisely the complex operationalization of the group interacts with actual perception is difficult to ascertain, but its logic, according to Krauss, can primarily be derived from the ground being rejected in favour of the instantaneity of the figure:

> For at the moment when the background of perceptual space — with its former status as reserve or secondariness — is rejected by modernism, in favor of the simultaneity that is understood as a precondition of vision, the logic of this inversion into not-ground already determines that new condition according to its mirror [...] relation to the diagonally opposite pole: figure [...]. The

> modernist not-ground is a field or background that has risen to the surface of the work to become exactly coincident with its foreground, a field that is thus ingested by the work as figure.[19]

What is of import to our understanding of focalization is Krauss's intriguing formulation of the three degrees of visibility of the figure that result from this surfacing of the ground. According to Krauss, modernism spurns the visible order of the figure embraced by the complex axis of perceptual vision in favour of the neutral, cognitive axis that yields a figure still visible, but 'unseen'; to this, Krauss adds a third order of the figure that 'operates beyond the reach of the visible' and works 'entirely underground, out of sight'. This order of the 'matrix' is largely aligned to the unconscious, and it materializes a ground, traditionally regarded to be neutral, as 'carnal and temporal'.[20]

In operationalizing the ambiguity of Rubin's spatio-temporal shift into a Klein group, Krauss effectively orders processes of looking into modes of visibility ('visible', 'unseen' and 'out of sight') and ushers the prepositional relation of figure and ground into one that is metaphorical. Yet in both approaches, the relation between figure and ground remains strongly tied to movements that operate between spaces of depiction and perception. In Rubin, this movement between perceiving different versions of the depicted has consequences on the vision retained in memory, while in Krauss this movement generates new levels of depiction that have consequences on different levels of figural visibility. In both, a primary figure-ground relation marked by 'against' yields new ways of seeing and narrativizing across time and space. Such a comparison, thus, provides a dynamic framework of focalizing figures in Beckett's and Giacometti's works.

Excavating and Evacuating Figures

One shared characteristic of the figures in Giacometti's Diego paintings and Beckett's radio plays *Embers* and *All That Fall*, is that they appear to be discovered and developed through processes of excavating. This is a result of depictive elements that give the impression of digging into the surface of the canvas or the voice, almost in an effort to find the figures from within or behind the ground, or to let them surface from beneath. In Giacometti's 1961 portrait of Diego (see figure 3.1), this takes the form of strokes that insistently obliterate or cancel out each other.

A close-up of the eyes reveals that the gaze of Diego has been represented by, as it were, emptying out the socket with repeated white strokes that interrupt each other in representing the curvature of the eye ball. As Giacometti has commented on more than one occasion, he does not represent the eye directly because he believes that:

> When you represent the eye precisely, you risk destroying exactly what you are after, namely the gaze. That's how it seems to me. There are very few artworks in which the gaze exists... In none of my sculptures since the war have I represented the eye precisely. I indicate the position of the eye. And I very often use a vertical line in place of the pupil. It's the curve of the eyeball one sees. And it gives the impression of the gaze. But that's where the problem

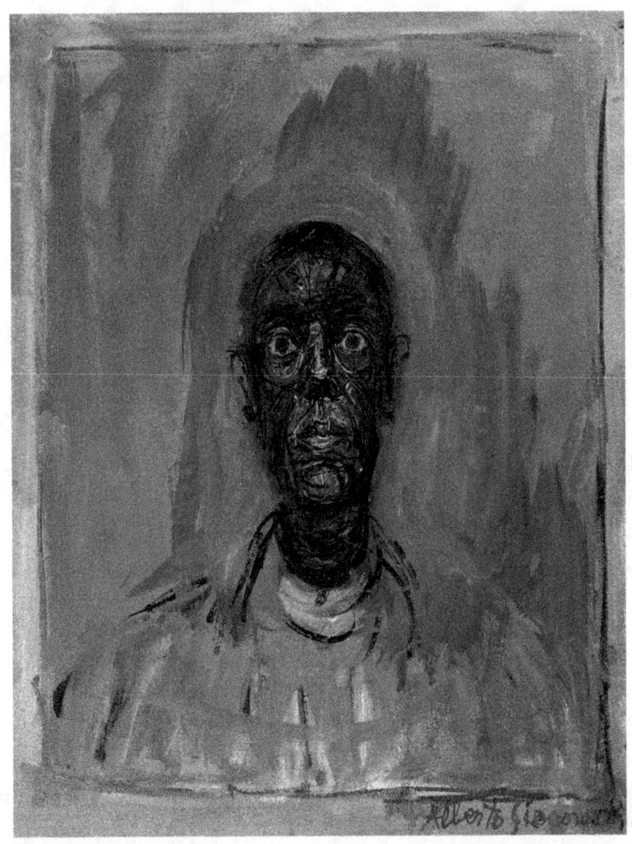

Fig. 3.1. Alberto Giacometti, *Head of Man*, 1961, oil on canvas, 45.1 × 35 cm, Museum of Fine Arts, Boston. © Succession Alberto Giacometti / Sabam, Belgium, 2022. Photo credit: Fondation Giacometti, Paris.

> comes in... When I get the curve of the eyeball right, then I've got the socket; when I get the socket, I've got the nostrils, the point of the nose, the mouth... and all of this together might just produce the gaze, without one's having to concentrate on the eye itself.[21]

Giacometti's eye is created from the exterior and through a further diffusion of its exteriority outwards, from the socket to the nostrils, and finally to the mouth. In other words, the gaze emerges as a form of residual impression constituted by the rest of the face. It is created through an emptying out of the face, which visually and physically — by way of the accumulation of paint around it — creates the impression of the gaze as a hollow on the canvas. This creates a central nebula in the portrait, and it replicates itself first in the black sphere of the head and then in the large, hastily-painted strokes that coat the head from its surroundings. The body takes a minor role and is rendered a shadowy impression, which further disembodies the head. Jean Soldini argues that this illusion of the figure emerging through a central nebula, or mist, constitutes the sense of a 'double of reality' because it erases the specificity of place without effacing its depth:

> Attorno alla figura vi è una sorta di nebulosa (nel mezzo della superficie della tela) da cui essa pare emergere. Segni bianchi attraversano il busto, togliendo solidità, capacità affermativa alla figura [...]. La figura, fermata in una fase decostruttiva (uso del bianco), è in bilico tra apparizione e sparizione, ma non perché Giacometti voglia suscitare un senso d'irrealtà. Quell'effetto costituisce un primo passo nella ricerca del 'doppio della realtà'. La nebulosa elimina ogni problema di luogo, è una sorta di 'profondità pura' da cui sale la figura.[22]

> [Around the figure there is a sort of mist (in the middle of the surface of the canvas) from which it seems to emerge. White marks traverse the bust, removing its solidity, but affirming the capacity of the figure [...]. The figure, arrested in a phase of deconstruction (through using white), hovers between appearance and disappearance, but this is not because Giacometti wants to create a sense of non-realism. This effect constitutes a first step in the search of a 'double of reality'. The mist eliminates any problem of place, and the figure rises from a sort of 'pure depth'.]

By using verbs such as 'emerge', 'hover' and 'rise', Soldini emphasizes a reading of the figure as one of movement rather than a materialization of vision. The face is not a given, but rather consists in the giving; the portrait of Diego is a portraiture of incessant excavating where the emptying out of the face is congruent with its making. The face emerges as a negative imprint where it is not only the gaze of Diego that emerges from the hollow of the canvas, but the gaze of Giacometti that is traced in the interruption of the lines that create the illusion of this hollow, or what Soldini terms the 'profondità pura'.

Interestingly, these portraits bear an uncanny resemblance to records of eye movements in facial recognition. In the 1960s, Alfred Yarbus, one of the founders of modern eye movement research, ran a series of experiments with his new miniature eye suction device known as 'the cap' to record the eye movements of his research participants on perceiving a variety of objects including photographs of faces.[23] His results were published in *Eye Movements and Vision* in 1967 (see figure 3.2).[24]

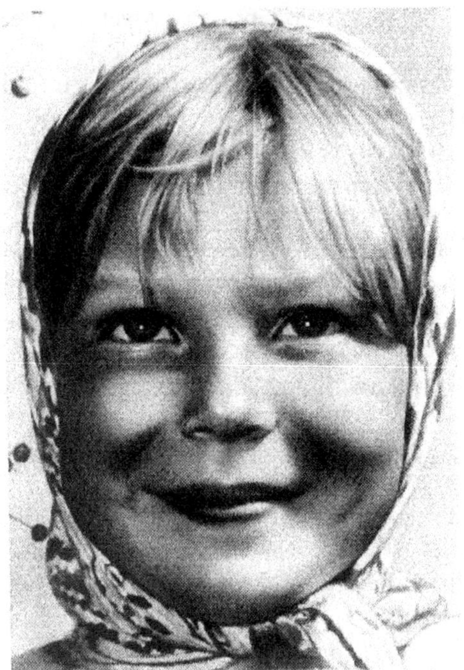

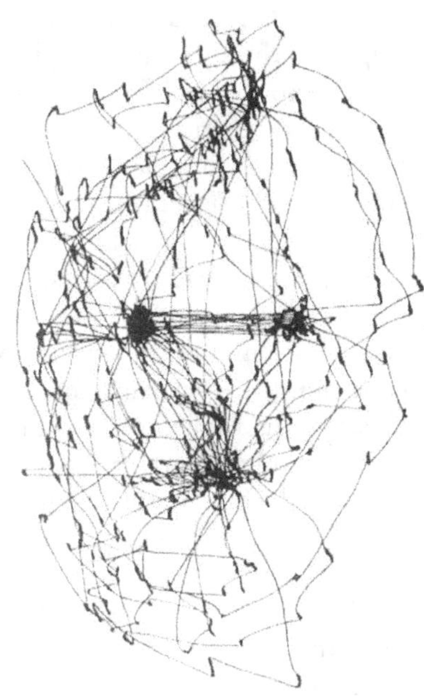

FIG. 3.2. Photograph of a girl's face ('Girl from the Volga' by S. Fridlyand) from the first page of the magazine *Ogonek*, 23 (1959), and corresponding record of the eye movements during free examination of the photograph with both eyes for three minutes. Image reproduced by permission of Springer Nature Customer Service Centre GmbH: Springer, *Eye Movements and Vision* by Alfred Yarbus, p. 180 (1967). Photo credit: Nicholas Wade.

Yarbus's records not only show that the eyes receive the most attention in an observer's reading of a face, but that such observation usually involves a cyclic, triangular alternation between the eyes, nose and mouth. Recalling figure 3.1, we likewise notice that these are the areas of the face that receive the most incessant re-working of strokes by Giacometti, and which preserve and coalesce the pathways of looking and remembering in so doing. Is the portrait of Diego perhaps both a writing and a retrieving of the face, and of memory? While Yarbus's records preserve the memory of looking at a face, Giacometti's paintings make a face which, upon being looked at, is already receding as memory. This recalls a particular incident when Giacometti stared intensely at his wife Annette after she had sat for him for the whole afternoon, because he realized he had not 'seen [her] all day'.[25] The memory of the face is, therefore, the face of memory and the face as memory: Giacometti's portraits evoke not just an excavating of the human figure through the brushstrokes, but inherently an excavating of interpretation that comes with all forms of reading and, here, a reading of the face. As Susan Sontag wrote in *Against Interpretation*, the 'modern style of interpretation excavates, and as it excavates, destroys; it digs "behind" the text, to find a sub-text which is the true one'.[26] Giacometti's drawing and re-drawing of his brother's face is, in this light, coalescent with the interpreting and re-interpreting of visual perception; to give memory a face is at the same time to reveal the face as memory.

Yarbus's cyclic scanning behaviour of facial perception brings up yet another interesting feature of Giacometti's portrait of Diego (figure 3.1): the use of white to triangulate the eyes, nose and mouth. As Soldini argues above, white marks across the torso not only affirm the capacity of the figure, but also arrest it in a phase of deconstruction. This phase, she posits, hovers between appearance and disappearance in a 'double of reality' that resists place. However, the white marks that constitute the face also give the impression of evacuating the figure: while excavating refers to a general sense of hollowing out (from *ex-*[out] + *cavare* [to hollow out], from *cavus* [cave]), evacuating takes on a stronger sense of emptying something out completely (from *evacuare*, 'to empty, make void, nullify', from *ex-* [out] + *vacuus* [empty]). A close look at another Diego portrait, the 1962 *Head of Diego* (see figure 3.3) reveals likewise that white strokes are integral to depicting the face, this time in delineating its contours.

It is an uncanny experience reading this portrait. Diego's eyes of dark, concentric meshwork draw our attention inwards, but the white strokes that highlight the forehead, ears, chin and neck constantly divert our attention outwards from the gaze. Our record of reading this portrait is perhaps very unlikely to resemble Yarbus's Volga girl as the interaction of the different strokes troubles the depth from or into which the face emerges. There is an ephemeral, destabilizing effect to reading the face precisely due to the white strokes that arrest, what Soldini calls, a phase of deconstruction. Is the blank beneath or within the figure, and by implication, is the face evacuated from or plunged into the void? 'I must paint the void ['le vide'] in front of me,' Giacometti says.[27] The void cannot be located, yet the void comes into place: here we are reminded of Nancy's *imago* (mentioned in Chapter 2), a place of displacement that weaves the absent into the present.

It should be mentioned that Giacometti's use of white to provoke questions of depth in perceiving faces and figures is not peculiar to these two works. It has been well established through the accounts of Giacometti's sitters, especially that of Isaku Yanaihara, that he painted with increasing whiteness on his canvas, even to the point of using white as complete erasure to paint the portrait all over again:

> Giacometti said to Yanaihara, according to his diary entry of 11 December, 'I can't understand how patiently you pose. It's madness.' The painting became whiter and whiter. The following day, Yanaihara recorded Giacometti as saying, 'For the first time, I'm beginning to really see'. But all that was in the picture was a grey circle. On their last day, 16 December, although there was only half an hour left, Yanaihara said, 'Shall we work, as usual?' Giacometti hesitated, but then said, 'Shall we try for just a little while?' 'With pleasure,' Yanaihara replied. The painting was completely erased and redone.[28]

The making of the face consists of a constant retreat from and erosion of it. This is a withdrawal that is realized on the canvas through the evacuation of white, on white, as white. The writing of the face is simultaneous but not coalescent with the writing of memory: when Soldini writes of a phase of deconstruction that is achieved through the use of white, it is perhaps this layering of white that arrests the figure between disappearance and appearance. Giacometti's struggle to see and

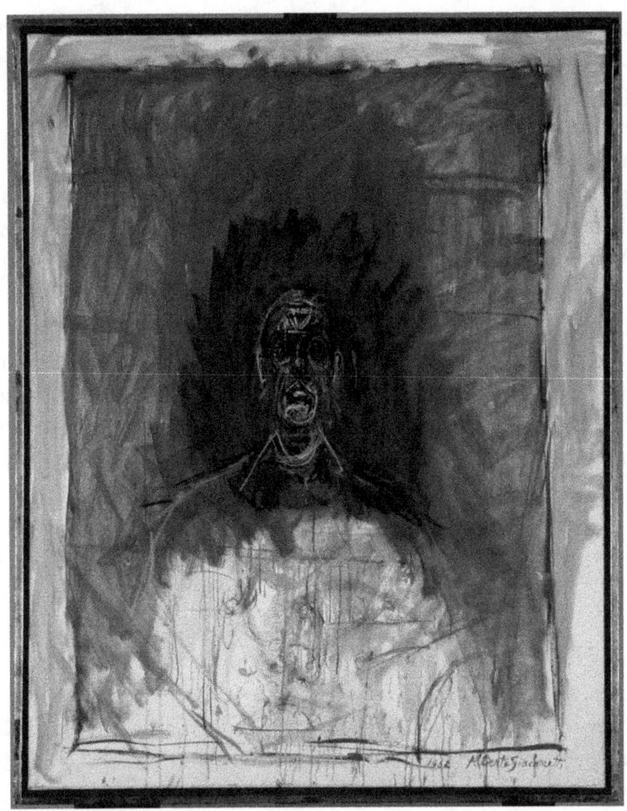

Fig. 3.3. Alberto Giacometti, *Head of Diego*, 1962, oil on canvas, 92 × 76 cm, Musée Granet, Aix-en-Provence. © Succession Alberto Giacometti / Sabam, Belgium, 2022. Photo credit: Fondation Giacometti, Paris.

make Diego's face culminates in a duration of erasure traced by the white on canvas. This is a blank that shows nothing, but, precisely, bears constantly the possibility of the disappearing returning.

In Beckett's *All That Fall* and *Embers*, this struggle to see is also a struggle to hear. The nature of the radio play depends on 'the whole thing's coming out of the dark', as Beckett is known to have written in one of his letters to Barney Rosset, his American publisher, in 1957.[29] But this 'thing' that comes out frequently remains a 'coming out' more than a 'thing', perhaps 'just another big, pale blur' as perceived of Mrs Rooney by Miss Fitt in *All That Fall*.[30] One of the reasons why movement becomes striking in the perception of both plays is due to the complexities of the voices: not only are they spoken on different levels of metaphysical existence — some appear to be internal thoughts as opposed to dialogue, for instance — but they are solely responsible for bringing about the entire existence of the characters, who are at the same time on different levels of mortal existence, that is, either living, dead or imaginary.

The voices of radio plays create figures and move bodies and, consequently, give the illusion of a story that continues. The nature of this figuration, however, also consists of methods of probing or digging into surfaces and grounds from which, or as which, figures seem to emerge. Here we are reminded of Beckett's letter to Kaun, in which he states the need to 'bore one hole after another in [language], until what lurks behind it — be it something or nothing — begins to seep through'.[31] Where Giacometti uses paint to recover and re-cover the human figure, Beckett uses voice, or more precisely, to borrow Max Eastman's phrase in describing the voice of prose, its 'fine traceries of related sound'.[32] The voices of these plays take on the imprint of the layering strokes of the brush, except that the canvas, as it were, is now solely in our heads and constantly expanded, at times disfigured and eventually almost erased.

There are two forms of digging associated with voices that are central to both plays. The first is concerned with probing the possibilities of the voice and the second with the possibilities of the story. There are two moments in *All That Fall* where the possibilities of voice are particularly humorously and tirelessly exhausted. The first occurs when Mrs Rooney meets Mr Tyler on the way to the station, and the second when Mr Tyler, Mr Barrell, Miss Fitt and Mrs Rooney are having a conversation before the train arrives:

> MR TYLER Come, Mrs Rooney —
>
> MRS ROONEY Go, Mr Tyler, go on and leave me, listening to the cooing of the ringdoves. [*Cooing.*] If you see my poor blind Dan tell him I was on my way to meet him when it all came over me again, like a flood. Say to him, Your poor wife, She told me to tell you it all came flooding over her again and... [*The voice breaks.*] ... she simply went back home... straight back home...
>
> MR TYLER Come, Mrs Rooney, come, the mail has not yet gone up, just take my free arm and we'll be there with time and to spare.
>
> MRS ROONEY [*Sobbing.*] What? What's all this now? [*Calmer.*] Can't you see I'm in trouble? [*With anger.*] Have you no respect for misery? [*Sobbing.*] Minnie! Little Minnie!

MR TYLER Come, Mrs Rooney, come, the mail has not yet gone up, just take my free arm and we'll be there with time and to spare.

MRS ROONEY [*Brokenly.*] In her forties now she'd be, I don't know, fifty, girding up her lovely little loins, getting ready for the change...

MR TYLER Come, Mrs Rooney, come, the mail —

MRS ROONEY [*Exploding.*] Will you get along with you, Mr Rooney, Mr Tyler I mean, will you get along with you now and cease molesting me?

[...]

MR TYLER You have lost your mother, Miss Fitt?

MISS FITT Good morning, Mr Tyler.

MR TYLER Good morning, Miss Fitt.

MISS FITT Good morning Mr Barrell.

MR BARRELL Good morning, Miss Fitt.

MR TYLER You have lost your mother, Miss Fitt?

MISS FITT She said she would be on the last train.

MRS ROONEY Do not imagine, because I am silent, that I am not present, and alive, to all that is going on.

MR TYLER [*To* Miss Fitt.] When you say the last train —

MRS ROONEY Do not flatter yourselves for one moment, because I hold aloof, that my sufferings have ceased. No. The entire scene, the hills, the plain, the racecourse with its miles and miles of white rails and three red stands, the pretty little wayside station, even you yourselves, yes, I mean it, and over all the clouding blue, I see it all, I stand here and see it all with eyes... [*The voice breaks.*] ... through eyes... oh if you had my eyes... you would understand... the things they have seen... and not looked away... this is nothing... nothing... what did I do with that handkerchief? [*Pause.*]

MR TYLER [*To* Miss Fitt.] When you say the last train — [Mrs Rooney *blows her nose violently and long.*] — when you say the last train, Miss Fitt, I take it you mean the twelve thirty.[33]

An initial reading of both passages would assume that we are listening to Mrs Rooney's thoughts in her head at the same time that we hear the voices of other characters being articulated in actual time and space. Mrs Rooney appears to be speaking to herself ('In her forties now she'd be, I don't know, fifty'), to the characters around and possibly within herself ('Go, Mr Tyler, go on and leave me'), to an imaginary audience within herself ('Do not flatter yourselves for one moment, because I hold aloof, that my sufferings have ceased. No.'), or to no particular person, not even herself ('through eyes... oh if you had my eyes... you would understand... the things they have seen... and not looked away'). Such multiplicity of voices within the same narrative frame is not a new concept. T. S. Eliot, for example, in *The Three Voices of Poetry*, argued that more than one voice is to be heard in a single poem:

> The first is the voice of the poet talking to himself — or to nobody. The second is the voice of the poet addressing an audience, whether large or small. The third is the voice of the poet when he attempts to create a dramatic character speaking in verse; when he is saying, not what he would say in his own person, but only what he can say within the limits of one character.[34]

Mrs Rooney's voice appears to take on the characteristics of all three types of voices, but further develops them by troubling the locus of its focalization. The repetition of the exact same lines of other characters interspersed with her voice begs the question of when these thoughts were spoken in her head. Mrs Rooney could not have had the time to go on to an exposition of Minnie or the landscape in the same time that Mr Tyler utters a single line. Are we, therefore, not listening to Mrs Rooney's voice in her head at that instant, but rather, overhearing the possibilities of her voice between that instant and its many other actual or imagined enumerations in time? Mrs Rooney appears to be speaking to no one, in a time neither past nor present, and in a space neither here nor there, inside nor outside. Just as Eliot had posited that 'part of our enjoyment of great poetry is the enjoyment of overhearing words which are not addressed to us', *All That Fall* presents a situation here of our overhearing words which, in their negation of both time and space, obliterates the possibility of the voice to address.[35]

This is a voice of Mrs Rooney that is caught between synchronic and diachronic time: the effect is that of a tape that has been stopped, rewound, but somehow played back differently each time. That 'somehow' evacuates Mrs Rooney's voice from any spatial or temporal specificity with a force analogous to the use of white that evacuates Diego from place and allows him to emerge from Soldini's 'profondità pura'. The central question shifts from when the voice is spoken to where the voice is coming from in relation to our hearing; because the presence of the voice is constantly receding, the figure which it makes is also held in a state of perpetual emerging. Mrs Rooney is, thus, perceived as a figure at once present and absent, made and unmade: she is perceived as a figure not only through exterior and interior voice, but through a form of mediatory voice that emerges from exhausting the possibilities of response in between. This emerging disfigures: she is given a voice at the same time that this voice is withdrawn from her through an evacuation of time and space.

This evacuation occurs because her voice, even though it is heard by the listener, does not seem to have gone out into any definable space and time. It defies the inherent paradox of the voice to come from and leave the same person, as explained by Steven Connor in *Dumbstruck: A Cultural History of Ventriloquism*:

> My voice comes from the inside of a body and radiates through a space which is exterior to and extends beyond that body. In moving from an interior to an exterior, and therefore marking out the relations of interior and exterior, a voice also announces and verifies the co-operation of bodies and the environments in which they have their being. The voice goes out into space, but also always, in its calling for a hearing, or the necessity of being heard, opens a space for itself to go out into, resound in, and return from. [...] If my voice is mine because it comes from me, it can only be known as mine because it also goes from me. My voice is, literally, my way of taking leave of my senses. What I say goes.[36]

With her huge range of expressions and sheer mass of a body, Mrs Rooney's voice clearly radiates through space, but it does not always 'go'. Because Mrs Rooney's voice removes itself from any demarcation of the inside and the outside, her figure thus hovers between appearing and disappearing. The voice is revealed as a passive receiver rather than active transmitter — here recalling the voice in *Texts for Nothing*

VIII referring to itself as 'a mere ventriloquist's dummy' or the narrator's line 'I say it as I hear it' in *How It Is*[37] — and together with the radio medium 'abolishes an individual's status as speaking being, observing [her] as an inert corpse'.[38] This is especially poignant when one realizes that it is only through Mrs Rooney's eyes — eyes that see but are not seen, as if through the eye-holes of a mask — that the listener gets a glimpse of the landscape where the scene takes place ('The entire scene, the hills, the plain, the racecourse with its miles and miles of white rails').[39] The viewer, thus, sees through the voice that is not heard: there is transference here of muteness, for this is a voice that at once gives a face to Mrs Rooney and disfigures it through a constant exhaustion of its possibilities in time and space as observed in the two scenes above.

While it is the interaction of voices that establishes the temporal and spatial presence of the characters in *All That Fall*, it is mainly Henry's voice that initiates our entry into the world of *Embers*, and it remains our main point of reference for most of the play. He creates all the remaining characters in the play (with, possibly, the exception of Ada) by way of stories that he tells in his own voice, or stories told in other voices but still framed through his. Yet, this figuration is once again perceived with a momentum of digging and emptying out, especially in relation to exhausting the possibilities of telling a story. According to Gidal, this sense of hollowing out in Beckett's works can be perceived as a kind of labour that consistently guards against meaning:

> Emptying the 'content' is a production, in language, towards nothing, towards not allowing any fullness to any word, phrase, sequence or sentence. The process goes against, extracting bit by bit from the words, remnants of 'content' mulled over and over, reified, finished with, emptied [...]. A fending against meaning, thus, not some transcendental totalism of 'emptiness' or 'fullness'. Rather than starting from a complete voiding of description, this writing of Beckett's places representation only in order to evacuate it, bit by bit, phrase by phrase, tortuously.[40]

While this is not unique to Beckett's radio plays, it is especially effective in this medium as the possibilities of focalization to evacuate representation extend to the immediate, aural employment of pauses, laughter and changes in narrative voice, all within a highly ambiguous and constantly shifting visual contextualization. In *Embers*, we can see all these at work in rendering impossible Henry's efforts to tell stories. One of the stories that Henry is obsessed with is that of Bolton and Holloway, which he begins to narrate three times but never finishes. It is on his third attempt that the possibilities of the story are most thoroughly voided. He begins this attempt suddenly while in the midst of talking about Ada taking the tram home after seeing his father:

> Takes tram home. [*Pause.*] Christ! [*Pause.*] 'My dear Bolton...' [*Pause.*] 'If it's an injection you want, Bolton, let down your trousers and I'll give you one, I have a panhysterectomy at nine,' meaning of course the anaesthetic. [*Pause.*] Fire out, bitter cold, white world, great trouble, not a sound. [*Pause.*] Bolton starts playing with the curtain, no, hanging, difficult to describe, draws it back no, kind of gathers it towards him and the moon comes flooding in, then lets it fall

> back, heavy velvet affair, and pitch black in the room, then towards him again, white, black, white, black, Holloway: 'Stop that for the love of God, Bolton, do you want to finish me?' [*Pause.*] Black, white, black, white, maddening thing.[41]

The story is established by three kinds of voices: Holloway's voice, a descriptive narrative voice that is constantly negated ('no, hanging, difficult to describe, draws it back no') and a more lyrical narrative voice that is made up of short phrases or single words that are repeated and alternated with rhythmic attention ('Fire out, bitter cold, white world, great trouble, not a sound'). These narrative voices draw the listener into a lull of story-telling, where the voice of the story-telling foregrounds the presence of the story-teller. The voices emerge one after the other from the same mouth that we cannot see: it is as if we were listening to a story in the dark, from the dark, or in Robert Frost's words, from 'voices behind a door that cuts off the words'.[42] This audibility of the voice as rhythm and expression is emphasized as the story continues, when both Henry's and Bolton's voices also enter the story:

> Then he suddenly strikes a match, Bolton does, lights a candle, catches it up above his head, walks over and looks Holloway full in the eye. [*Pause.*] Not a word, just the look, the old blue eye, very glassy, lids worn thin, lashes gone, whole thing swimming, and the candle shaking over his head. [*Pause.*] Tears? [*Pause. Long laugh.*] Good God no! [*Pause.*] Not a word, just the look, the old blue eye, Holloway: 'If you want a shot say so and let me get the hell out of here.' [*Pause.*] 'We've had this before, Bolton, don't ask me to go through it again.' [*Pause.*] Bolton: 'Please!' [*Pause.*] 'Please!' [*Pause.*] 'Please, Holloway!'[43]

Henry's voice, which emerges as a question and a laugh (his only long successful laugh in the play following a previous failure to laugh in the presence of Ada), pries open the story to reveal his presence as story-teller: the neutral ground shifts momentarily to become not-ground. We are no longer privy to the story behind closed doors because the mouth that tells the story betrays the voice — the laugh cracks through the voice as an open mouth — and the 'abstract sound of sense' is broken.[44] The voice, as it were, no longer delivers the 'posture proper to the sentence', and what we experience is less a lull of story-telling than a consternation of voices.[45] The five voices start to collapse onto one another, and the story takes on not the shape of the words, but the shape of their interruption as told by the pleading mouth that has come out of the dark:

> Candle shaking and guttering all over the place, lower now, old arm tired and takes it in the other hand and holds it high again, that's it, that always was it, night, and the embers cold, and the glim shaking in your old fist, saying, Please! Please! [*Pause.*] Begging. [*Pause.*] Of the poor. [*Pause.*] Ada! [*Pause.*] Father! [*Pause.*] Christ! [*Pause.*] Holds it high again, naughty world, fixes Holloway, eyes drowned, won't ask again, just the look, Holloway covers his face, not a sound, white world, bitter cold, ghastly scene, old men, great trouble, no good. [*Pause.*] No good. [*Pause.*] Christ![46]

These increasing exhortations and exclamations emphasize the corporeality of the voice as it becomes increasingly difficult for the listener to make out where vocal representation stops and vocal expressions take over: when is an exclamation a diegetic marker rather than a mimetic expression? At what point is Henry the narrator or the narrated? Words are emptied out of Henry; they interrupt his voice as anxious pleas for names, people and absences ('Ada! [*Pause.*] Father! [*Pause.*] Christ!'). The narrative takes on the shape of its interruption: Bolton's plea conflates with Henry's ('Please! Please! [*Pause.*] Begging. [*Pause.*] Of the poor. [*Pause.*] Ada! [*Pause.*]') at the same time that both the descriptive and more lyrical narrative voices start stumbling into each other ('Holloway covers his face, not a sound, white world, bitter cold, ghastly scene, old men, great trouble'). The voices no longer pry apart, the story becomes the texture and the erosion of its being interrupted, and the mouth surfaces into the light; it is 'no good', finished.

Just as the voice that delivered the story was gradually emptied out of it, the figures that were created by Henry's voice were gradually withdrawn into the hollow of the mouth that surfaced from the 'tortuous' disfiguration of such an interruption. The story cannot continue because the story — in its production towards emptiness, as it were — is withdrawn into its own singular space once its possibilities are voided. This space, which had become the site of such substitutions and repetitions in the act of story-telling, is also the site of withdrawal, of a digging in, that reveals the voice as a kind of wound:

> Contrapuntal theory or a procession of stigmata: a wound no doubt comes in (the) place of the point signed by singularity, in (the) place of its very instant (*stigmē*), at its point, its tip. But *in (the) place of* this event, place is given over, for the same wound, to substitution, which repeats itself there, retaining of the irreplaceable only a past desire.[47]

The mouth comes 'in the place of' the voice as a corporeal, spatial substitution of a narration that cannot be finished; there is no figure to be found in the ground, and only a semblance to be found in that digging as a retrieval of the already left, the 'given over'. As Lea Sinoimeri has pointed out, Henry's going on depends on a 'dramatic alterity' between an inner voice that he has rejected and an outer voice that lends itself to animating the character of his story; with the tormented erosion of this alterity as the play progresses, Henry 'loses all his powers'.[48] Henry in giving the story a voice, therefore, subjects his own voice to a disavowal with the words it articulates: the words of memory become the memory of words, the memory as word. The traces of figure-making align with the movements of writing the figure as face and memory. They retain not the perception itself, but the memory of this perceiving. And because this memory exists between presence and non-presence, a given and an excavated, it has not yet arrived, but is a form of anamnesis which always 'remains to come'.[49]

Doubled Focalizations

Another way in which the radio plays and the Diego paintings play with the focalization of figures is through the use of doubled frames which also interrogate subjectivity through figure-ground relations. In *Embers*, this takes the form of a framed narrative, of which the most compelling is Henry and Ada's love-making which Henry recalls as he stands by the edge of the water:

> HENRY I thought I might try and get as far as the water's edge. [*Pause. With a sigh.*] And back. [*Pause.*] Stretch my old bones.
> [*Pause.*]
> ADA Well, why don't you? [*Pause.*] Don't stand there thinking about it. [*Pause.*] Don't stand there staring. [*Pause. He goes towards the sea. Boots on shingle, say ten steps. He halts at water's edge. Pause. Sea a little louder. Distant.*] Don't wet your good boots.
> [*Pause.*]
> HENRY Don't, don't...
> [*Sea suddenly rough.*]
> ADA [*Twenty years earlier, imploring.*] Don't! Don't!
> HENRY [*Ditto, urgent.*] Darling!
> ADA [*Ditto, more feebly.*] Don't!
> HENRY [*Ditto, exultantly.*] Darling!
> [*Rough sea.* Ada *cries out. Cry and sea amplified, cut off. End of evocation. Pause. Sea calm. He goes back up deeply shelving beach. Boots laborious on shingle. He halts. Pause. He moves on. He halts. Pause. Sea calm and faint.*]
> ADA Don't stand there gaping. Sit down.[50]

Unlike Henry's telling of Bolton and Holloway's story wherein his voice creates figures that are absent, in this instance, his voice is given over to voices that, in turn, create figures that are twice-absent. These entities are twice-absent because they only exist in the sphere of Henry's memory, and in being heard in their own right — Ada is heard as Ada's voice, unlike Bolton who was heard through Henry's voice — take on the paradoxical image of a ghost turned inside-out. This impression is a result of hearing a mimetic voice that, by the logic of the doubled frame narrative, should exist completely on the level of the diegetic. Ada's voice undercuts this logic and is focalized through a peculiar in-between space of mimesis and diegesis. While the movement of giving and excavating previously explicated seemed to arrest the figure between appearing and disappearing, the effect of this doubled framing is one of perpetual oscillation between seeing and speaking, mask and voice.

This effect of oscillation is sensitively explored through the chilling, yet moving image of Nancy's 'Oscillator'. Oscillation, in Nancy's account, derives its sense from a perpetuation of 'betweens' founded on the 'doubled' and 'incommunicable' nature of vision and speech:

> This word ['oscillator'] is the diminutive form of the Latin *os*, which signifies the mouth and, by metonymy, the face. *Oscillum* thus designated a small mouth (closely related to *osculum*, kiss), as well as a small mask of Bacchus hung in the vines as a scarecrow: the movement of this face swinging in the wind produced the sense of 'oscillation.' The Oscillator, then, swings between mouth and face, between speech and vision, between the emission of sense and the reception of form. But what appears to move toward an encounter does not do so at all: on the contrary, the mouth and the look are turned forward and are parallel, turned into the distance, toward an infinite perpetuation of their double and incommunicable position. Between mouth and eye, the entire face oscillates.[51]

The figure of Ada, then, is one that appears to hover between mouth and mask, speech and vision. The single word 'don't' that we hear from her in the episode quoted above gives her face the hollow of the mouth, the depth of that plea, as it were, which at the same time perpetuates the utter muteness of the mask that she wears only through Henry's memory. Like the Oscillator that 'wants to make the mask speak and [...] wants to give speech a mask', the doubled framing gives the absent figure a voice and a face which seem to oscillate but never conflate.[52] Thus the Oscillator keeps swinging; Ada remains always to come.

But pushing this further, the doubled focalization of Ada in a space between mimesis and diegesis also creates a figure that, in its oscillating, leads the listener through an experience of ruin. According to Derrida, the ruin is experience *itself*; it is memory laid bare and open like a hollow:

> The ruin is not in front of us; it is neither a spectacle nor a love object. It is experience itself [...] Ruin is, rather, this memory open like an eye, or like the hole in a bone socket that lets you see without showing you anything *at all*, anything *of the all*. This, *for* showing you *nothing at all*, *nothing of the all*. 'For' means here both *because* the ruin shows *nothing at all* and *with a view to* showing *nothing of the all*.[53]

This is interesting when examined in the context of a radio play because the radio medium has the capacity to enter and exit an embedded narrative with minimal diegetic intervention; such an option of directly embedding voices within voices would not have been possible on an actual stage without explicit diegetic interference or indication. This means that radio has a much greater potential to 'show' rather than to 'tell', which in the case of Ada's narrative framed through Henry, creates both the perception of 'nothing', to use Derrida's terminology, and the diegesis of 'showing' the 'nothing'. Like a bomb-site which at once irrevocably destroys and therefore immortalizes the past, Ada shows up because she has been rendered strikingly absent. In this sense, Ada appears to be made and unmade by way of both perception and depiction.

In *All That Fall*, a different type of doubled framing in the form of sound, rather than voice, is used to great effect. This can be found at the start and end of the play, where a prolonged section of sound effects can be heard:

> Rural sounds. Sheep, bird, cow, cock, severally, then together.
> *Silence.*
> Mrs Rooney *advances along country road towards railway station. Sound of her dragging feet.*
> *Music faint from house by way. 'Death and the Maiden.'*
> *The steps slow down, stop.*
> [...]
> *Silence.* Jerry *runs off. His steps die away. Tempest of wind and rain. It abates. They move on. Dragging steps, etc. They halt. Tempest of wind and rain.*[54]

Sound can be seen as the frame narrative to *All That Fall* in the same way as Henry is to *Embers*. Sound contains, structures and embodies the play from which the narrative is subsequently told and into which it is eventually withdrawn. The frame narrator, in this case, has no words; it is mute but not silent, for it not only evokes the depth of the space at the start (animals, countryside, an old lady, the music of Schubert), it also revokes the time of the place at the end when the carefully choreographed alternation and repetition of steps, wind and rain, and silence suggest a perpetual continuation and dissolution of time.

This perpetuation is not only of time, but also of ruin, in Derrida's sense of the word. The tragedy of what happened on the train is revealed at the end of the play through Jerry's words ('It was a little child fell out of the carriage, Ma'am. [*Pause.*] On to the line, Ma'am. [*Pause.*] Under the wheels, Ma'am.'), but it is subsumed and eclipsed into this deliberately choreographed rhythm of sounds that closes the play.[55] The story is told twice and the boy falls twice: first through voice and second through sound; first onto the tracks and second into oblivion. The doubled framing here reveals ruin not only as experience but as dissolution of both memory and self:

> Ruin is the self-portrait, this face looked at in the face as the memory of itself [...] The figure, the face, then sees its visibility being eaten away; it loses its integrity without disintegrating. For the incompleteness of the visible monument comes from the eclipsing structure of the *trait*, from a structure that is only remarked, pointed out, impotent or incapable of being reflected in the shadow of the self-portrait. So many reversible propositions. For one can just as well read the pictures of ruins as the figures of a portrait, indeed, of a self-portrait.[56]

The visibility of the boy who fell is dissolved through sound but incompletely so, and it remains a 'lingering dissolution', in Mrs Rooney's words.[57] This incompleteness is precisely what constitutes the experience of tragedy as ruin, for it perpetuates, in all who witness and remain, the figuration and the reversibility of the falling before themselves, upon themselves, onto themselves: focalization reverses its looking upon the listener. This is a form of ruinous chasm which the dead fall into and from which the living shall continue to live. As James Boswell records the words of Gerard Hamilton upon learning of Samuel Johnson's death:

> He has made a chasm, which not only nothing can fill up, but which nothing has a tendency to fill up. Johnson is dead. Let us go to the next best: — there is nobody; no man can be said to put you in mind of Johnson.[58]

Johnson's death, like the little boy's falling, is not framed once, but twice. The compounded silence of that doubled framing through Boswell and Hamilton is to be found in the space of the dash, which at once perpetuates and fractures the blank of death's aftermath. But more than that, for this blank is triply framed, on Boswell's page, through the unbearable suffusion of the footnotes which almost push the 'main' text out of the margins of the page. Perhaps these graphic transformations of the blank, which like a ruin lying open as an eye socket, speak of the struggle to translate the loss which cannot be fulfilled simply by uttering 'Johnson is dead' or 'On to the line, Ma'am. Under the wheels, Ma'am'. Here then, in both Boswell's dash and *All That Fall's* final sound sequence of wind, rain and steps, we experience a silent scene of falling. In the reflection of the dissolving figure of the boy who falls, those who look on will look on in silence, all who remain find their faces in all that fall. Sound, in this form of doubled framing, reveals memory as a suture that cannot close the incision of ruin.

In Giacometti's paintings, we observe this ruin through the use of the double frame which likewise enacts a reversibility and oscillation between the inside and outside of the portrait, and by extension the subjectivity between the figure and the artist/viewer, between looking and being looked at. Most of the figures in the

Diego portraits exist within a frame interior to the painting's frame. The interior frames are usually the only straight cut lines with a linear orientation amidst the portrait's circularity. The evocation here is of a portrait within the portrait, where the space of the portrait is circumscribed not as depth but surface. The excavation of the interiority of the figure is in tandem with the evacuation of any pretence of depth in the canvas. But since the interior frame is painted against both the exterior frame and the interior portrait, when does it cease being part of the internal portrait and start being part of the external frame? Is it a supplement to the portrait or to the frame? The question expresses the nature of oscillation inherent in the painted frame: it is neither clearly inside nor outside, but rather, a figure in its own right, one which has the capacity to reverse the inside upon the outside, and vice versa.

Derrida would call this figure the *parergon*, a term derived from Kant's 'General Remarks' to the second edition of *Der Religion innerhalb der Grenzen der bloßen Vernunft* [Religion Within the Limits of Reason Alone].[59] Derrida adopts this term in *La Vérité en peinture* [The Truth in Painting] to refer to a structure that is integral to the body of a work (the *ergon*) yet detachable from it (he makes the distinction that the column would be a *parergon* but not the site chosen for the erection of a temple). The *parergon* is thus 'a hybrid of outside and inside, but a hybrid which is not a mixture or a half-measure, an outside which is called to the inside of the inside in order to constitute it as an inside'.[60] The frame of a painting is thus a *parergon* because it is at once integral to the painting and yet stands apart from it, exterior enough to be detachable from the painting and yet interior enough to expose a lack in the unity of the painting if it is detached:

> What constitutes them as *parerga* is not simply their exteriority as surplus, it is the internal structural link which rivets them to the lack in the interior of the *ergon*. And this lack would be constitutive of the very unity of the *ergon*. Without this lack, the *ergon* would have no need of a *parergon*. The *ergon*'s lack is the lack of a *parergon*, of the garment or the column which nevertheless remains exterior to it.[61]

Derrida goes on to explain that this exteriority of the *parergon* is constituted by its standing out against both the canvas and the wall, but a standing out that takes the nature of an effacing:

> The *parergon* stands out [*se détache*] both from the *ergon* (the work) and from the milieu, it stands out first of all like a figure on a ground [...] the parergonal frame stands out against two grounds [*fonds*], but with respect to each of those two grounds, it merges [*se fond*] into the other. With respect to the work which can serve as a ground for it, it merges into the work which stands out against the general background. There is always a form on a ground, but the *parergon* is a form which has as its traditional determination not that it stands out but that it disappears, buries itself, effaces itself, melts away at the moment it deploys its greatest enemy. The frame is in no case a background in the way that the milieu or the work can be, but neither is its thickness as margin a figure. Or at least it is a figure which comes away of its own accord [*s'enlève d'elle-même*].[62]

The *parergon* is what gives the work an element of its unity that is otherwise absent, but it is an element which remains invisible in its giving and is easily withdrawn.

Giacometti's painted frame is, however, forcibly demarcated and has no intention of disappearing or melting away, simply by virtue of its sharing the same pictorial space as the figure. It is a negative imprint of the *parergon*: rather than melting away or effacing itself, the painted frame merges against the interior and the exterior, and creates a doubled space within the portrait precisely by eradicating any pretence of depth inherent in the canvas. This is similar to the use of multiple frames in many of Francis Bacon's paintings of around the same time, for instance the use of cages enclosing the figure in *Study for Portrait* (1971); but whereas Bacon's multiple frames generally interrogate the possibility of ever embedding the figure, and by extension the self, Giacometti's doubled frames reveal rather than confront this lack of selfhood.[63]

The doubled space becomes a graphic excavation of an interior excavating: it is the blank mask of the nothing of Derrida's ruin that shows up in the making of the figure. The viewer perceives the portrait of Diego in its opaque flatness just as the making of Diego's figure by Giacometti — or more precisely the memory of the writing of him — is the experience of ruin that lets one see without showing one anything. The doubled *parergon* reverses the interior excavating into the exterior excavation; it places the inside and the outside in perpetual oscillation, and thus transfers the figure-making to the viewer. We no longer know if it is the ground of the figure that has been rendered flat, or our looking into our picture that has been limited, curtailed and interrupted. In looking through a conventional framed painting we see what is behind the Albertian window, but in looking through a doubly-framed painting we see that what is behind the window is a mirror. In his poem 'Self-portrait in a Convex Mirror', John Ashbery writes of this portrait/mirror (in reference to Parmigianino's painting of the same title) as a collapsing structure of reflections through a simultaneous use of repetition and enjambment, which evoke a coalescent sense of inversion in symmetry:

> Chiefly his reflection, of which the portrait
> Is the reflection, of which the portrait
> Is the reflection once removed.[64]

The eye seeks its pupil; the canvas laid bare like the socket of the eye gives us nothing of and nothing but the reflection of the *pupa* (a girl, a doll) from which the 'pupil' is derived. But the *pupa* in turn gives us 'puppet', and the reflection of the *pupa* is once again subjected to another reflection, hung on ropes, moved by strings, before an audience, onto us. The last substitution in Derrida's procession of stigmata is ultimately the blankness of (our) looking; figure-making is complete, passed on, starts over. In the effacement, replacements and repetitions of frames upon grounds, and grounds into figures, focalization dissolves and reveals the given and the remembered as ruin and wound, thus circulating the absent yet leaving it empty; it remains to come. And it is perhaps on this thought that *Krapp's Last Tape* ends, when Krapp sits before his voice like his own ventriloquist's puppet, and the silence of the past dissolves into the silence of the present, and in so doing, gives the present its silent face of the future: 'Perhaps my best years are gone. When there was a chance of happiness. But I wouldn't want them back. Not with the fire in me now. No, I wouldn't want them back. [Krapp *motionless staring before him. The tape runs on in silence*]'.[65]

Notes to Chapter 3

1. Aulus Gellius, *Attic Nights*, I, 287.
2. See for example, Mieke Bal and Jane E. Lewin, 'The Narrating and the Focalizing: A Theory of the Agents in Narrative', *Style*, 17 (1983), 234–69; Gerald Prince, 'A Point of View on Point of View or Refocusing Focalization', in *New Perspectives on Narrative Perspective*, ed. by Willie van Peer and Seymour Chatman (Albany: State University of New York Press, 2001), pp. 43–50; Seymour Benjamin Chatman, *Story and Discourse: Narrative Structure in Fiction and Film* (Ithaca, NY: Cornell University Press, 1980); Manfred Jahn, 'Windows of Focalization: Deconstructing and Reconstructing a Narratological Concept', *Style*, 30 (1996), 241; David Herman, 'Hypothetical Focalization', *Narrative*, 2 (1994), 230–53.
3. Genette, *Narrative Discourse*, pp. 186, 188.
4. Ibid. p. 189.
5. Samuel Beckett, *Embers*, in *The Complete Dramatic Works*, pp. 251–64 (p. 257).
6. See for example Susana Herrera Damas, 'The Roles of the Narrator in Radio Features', *Recherches en Communication*, 37 (2013), 73–80; Emma Rodero, 'Stimulating the Imagination in a Radio Story: The Role of Presentation Structure and the Degree of Involvement of the Listener', *Journal of Radio & Audio Media*, 19 (2012), 45–60; Bartosz Lutostański, 'A Narratology of Radio Drama: Voice, Perspective, Space', *Audionarratology: Interfaces of Sound and Narrative*, 52 (2016), 117.
7. Mieke Bal and Sherry Marx-MacDonald, *Travelling Concepts in the Humanities: A Rough Guide* (Toronto: University of Toronto Press, 2002). Bal's engagement with focalization spans most of her works. It first appeared in response to Gérard Genette's typology, and her distinction of the term in narratology remains marked from Genette's. See Genette; Bal and Lewin. For Bal's development of the term in later works, and increasingly through visual works, see for example Mieke Bal, *Quoting Caravaggio*; *Narratology: Introduction to the Theory of Narrative*, trans. by Christine van Boheeman (Toronto: University of Toronto Press, 2009); *The Mottled Screen: Reading Proust Visually*, trans. by Anna Louise Milne (Stanford, CA: Stanford University Press, 1997); and *Double Exposures: The Subject of Cultural Analysis* (New York: Routledge, 1996).
8. Bal and Marx-MacDonald, *Travelling Concepts in the Humanities*, p. 39.
9. Bal, *The Mottled Screen*, p. 265.
10. Benveniste, 'Subjectivity in Language'.
11. Bal and Marx-MacDonald, *Travelling Concepts in the Humanities*, pp. 41, 43.
12. Ibid., p. 43.
13. Steven Connor, '"I Switch Off": The Ordeals of Radio', in *Beckett, Modernism and the Material Imagination* (Cambridge: Cambridge University Press, 2014), pp. 65–83 (p. 67).
14. Samuel Beckett, *Murphy*, ed. by J. C. C. Mays (London: Faber & Faber, 2009), p. 4; William James, *The Principles of Psychology* [1890], 2 vols, (New York: Henry Holt, 1918), I, 488.
15. James Elkins, *On Pictures and the Words That Fail Them* (Cambridge: Cambridge University Press, 1998), p. 120.
16. Rubin's vase first appeared in his dissertation *Synsoplevede Figurer* in 1915. For translated portions of his dissertation, see Edgar Rubin, 'Figure and Ground', in *Readings in Perception*, ed. by M. Wertheimer and David C. Beardslee (Princeton, NJ: D. Van Nostrand, 1958), pp. 194–203.
17. Rosalind E. Krauss, *The Optical Unconscious* (Cambridge, MA: MIT Press, 1993), p. 14.
18. Ibid. p. 19.
19. Ibid. p. 24.
20. Ibid. pp. 217, 192.
21. Interview with Alberto Giacometti recorded for the film *Alberto Giacometti*, dir. by Ernst Scheidegger (Zurich, 1966).
22. Jean Soldini, *Alberto Giacometti: la somiglianza introvabile* (Milan: Jaca Book, 1998), p. 139.

23. An introduction to the significance of Yarbus's work on modern eye movement research, and especially cognitive influences on face viewing, can be found in Benjamin W. Tatler and others, 'Yarbus, Eye Movements, and Vision', *i-Perception*, 1.1 (2010), 7–27.
24. Alfred L. Yarbus, *Eye Movements and Vision*, trans. by Basil Haigh (New York: Springer Science & Business Media, 1967).
25. Michael Peppiatt, *Alberto Giacometti in Postwar Paris* (New Haven, CT: Yale University Press, 2001), p. 13.
26. Susan Sontag, *Against Interpretation, and Other Essays* (New York: Farrar, Straus & Giroux, 1966), p. 6.
27. Giacometti cited in Takeda, '"An Unknown Country"', p. 194.
28. Ibid., p. 198.
29. Beckett quoted in Kalb, 'The Radio and Television Plays, and "Film"', p. 129.
30. Samuel Beckett, *All That Fall*, in *The Complete Dramatic Works*, pp. 169–200 (p. 183).
31. Beckett, *Disjecta*, p. 172.
32. Max Eastman, *Colors of Life: Poems and Songs and Sonnets* (New York: Alfred A. Knopf, 1918), p. 33.
33. Beckett, *All That Fall*, pp. 176, 185.
34. T. S. Eliot, *The Three Voices of Poetry* (Cambridge: Cambridge University Press, 1955), p. 4.
35. Ibid. p. 21.
36. Steven Connor, *Dumbstruck: A Cultural History of Ventriloquism* (Oxford: Oxford University Press, 2000), pp. 6–7.
37. Samuel Beckett, *Texts for Nothing VIII*, in *Collected Shorter Prose: 1945–1980* (London: Calder, 1986), p. 97; *How It Is* (London: Calder, 1985), p. 7.
38. Llewellyn Brown, *Beckett, Lacan and the Voice* (Stuttgart: ibidem, 2016), p. 258.
39. Beckett, *All That Fall*, p. 185.
40. Gidal, *Understanding Beckett*, pp. 49–50.
41. Beckett, *Embers*, pp. 263–64.
42. Robert Frost, *Selected Letters of Robert Frost*, ed. by Lawrance R. Thompson (New York: Holt, Rinehart & Winston, 1964), p. 80.
43. Beckett, *Embers*, p. 264.
44. Frost, *Selected Letters of Robert Frost*, p. 80.
45. Ibid.
46. Beckett, *Embers*, p. 264.
47. Jacques Derrida, 'The Deaths of Roland Barthes', in *The Work of Mourning*, ed. by Pascale-Anne Brault and Michael Naas (Chicago, IL: University of Chicago Press, 2001), pp. 31–68 (p. 67).
48. Lea Sinoimeri, '"Close your eyes and listen to it": Schizophonia and Ventriloquism in Beckett's Plays', *Miranda*, 4 (2011) <http://journals.openedition.org/miranda/1924> [accessed 9 August 2021.
49. Ibid.
50. Beckett, *Embers*, pp. 259–60.
51. Nancy, *The Ground of the Image*, p. 73.
52. Ibid.
53. Jacques Derrida, *Memoirs of the Blind: The Self-portrait and Other Ruins*, trans. by Pascale-Anne Brault and Michael Naas (Chicago, IL: University of Chicago Press, 1993), p. 69.
54. Beckett, pp. 172, 199.
55. Ibid.
56. Derrida, *Memoirs of the Blind*, p. 68.
57. Beckett, *All That Fall*, p. 175.
58. James Boswell, *The Life of Samuel Johnson*, 4 vols (London: Cadell & Davies, 1816), IV, 464.
59. Immanuel Kant, *Der Religion innerhalb der Grenzen der bloßen Vernunft*, 2nd edn (Königsberg: Nicolovius, 1794).
60. Jacques Derrida, *The Truth in Painting*, trans. by Geoff Bennington and Ian McLeod (Chicago, IL: University of Chicago Press, 1987), p. 63.
61. Ibid. pp. 59–60.

62. Ibid. p. 61.
63. Alphen, *Francis Bacon and the Loss of Self*, p. 162.
64. John Ashbery, 'Self-portrait in a Convex Mirror', *Poetry*, 124 (1974), 247–61.
65. Beckett, *Krapp's Last Tape*, in *The Complete Dramatic Works*, pp. 213–24 (p. 223).

CONCLUSION

> Cleverly, by Heaven! And wittily, in my opinion, does Gavius Bassus explain the derivation of the word *persona*, in the work that he composed *On the Origin of Words*; for he suggests that that word is formed from *personare*. 'For,' he says, 'the head and the face are shut in on all sides by the covering of the persona, or mask, and only one passage is left for the issue of the voice; and since this opening is neither free nor broad, but sends forth the voice after it has been concentrated and forced into one single means of egress, it makes the sound clearer and more resonant. Since then that covering of the face gives clearness and resonance to the voice, it is for that reason called persona, the o being lengthened because of the formation of the word.'
>
> — Aulus Gellius, *Attic Nights*, Book 5[1]

The play *Mon père, Giacometti* (2014) features an elderly painter whose dementia increasingly leaves him confused about his own identity.[2] He begins to believe that he is Giacometti, whom he has admired throughout his life, and begins to paint portraits in the same style as him. He also begins to mistake his son for Isaku Yanaihara, the Japanese philosophy professor who was one of Giacometti's most important male models. The painter makes his son Noriyuki sit for his portraits, and in the process of painting begins to speak French to him, sometimes in an extremely agitated fashion. His son, wanting to understand him better, begins to learn French, but never finds himself capable of responding adequately to his father when he was in the state of Giacometti. One day he stumbles upon Yanaihara's writings on Giacometti, and realizes that the French lines his father has been speaking are taken from these writings. He begins memorizing Yanaihara's replies from the same book and transposes them into his sittings with his father, thus giving his father's drawn lines, their spoken lines and their time together, a way of continuing. By speaking Yanaihara's words, Noriyuki adopts a voice, face and posture recognized by his father in spite of and due to his forgetting; this is a forgetting now written out by remembering lines of words, of relations and of a history thus reclaimed by a delusion no more delusive or real than theatre and dementia.

Written, directed and performed by Noriyuki Kiguchi with his own father Keizo Kiguchi (who is in reality a painter), *Mon père, Giacometti* has been performed in six cities in Japan and Switzerland since its debut in 2014. One of the most moving moments of the play is Noriyuki's stumbling upon Yanaihara's writings — this chance encounter allowed him to temporarily reconcile the image of his father, whom he was gradually losing to dementia, with a face and a voice thus fixated as text. But where do this face and voice come from, if not from the writings of a man who was likewise attempting to hold on to and make sense of time and memory?

Much is now known by Giacometti scholars outside Japan of Isaku Yanaihara, but what is less said, and which strikes me as particularly interesting, is the way their meeting involved missed beats and coincidences.[3] Yanaihara had spotted Giacometti on two occasions around Montparnasse in 1955 but did not speak to him for fear of troubling such a celebrity: 'les œuvres se suffisaient à elles-mêmes' [the works were enough in themselves], he told himself.[4] It was only upon looking at one of Giacometti's paintings in an art gallery at the end of October that year — 'que je contemplais ce violent enchevêtrement de noirs et blancs qui se détachaient d'un néant couleur de cendre' [contemplating the violent entanglement of blacks and whites that were detached from a nothingness of ash] — that Yanaihara suddenly felt an impulse to meet him.[5] The gallery declined to give Yanaihara the studio address of Giacometti, but offered to pass him a message; a meeting ensued on 8 November 1955,[6] as did 230 sittings and a large number of portraits over the next six years,[7] a period that Hohl and other scholars have termed Giacometti's 'second artistic crisis'.[8] Yanaihara wrote about his friendship with Giacometti both in French and Japanese.[9] Of particular importance are 完本 ジャコメッティ手帖 I and II [The Complete Giacometti Handbooks I and II], which in 800 pages detail the sittings down to the very words of the conversations between the two, and which played a vital part in the introduction of Giacometti to Japan.[10]

Montparnasse was, of course, also the setting for the start of Beckett and Giacometti's friendship. This lasted almost three decades until Giacometti's death in 1966, a loss which evidently distressed Beckett, as seen in his words written to Jacoba van Velde: 'Giacometti mort. Devine mort. Oui, conduis-moi au Père Lachaise, en brûlant les feux rouges' [Giacometti dead. Devine dead. Yes, drive me to Père Lachaise, blazing through the red lights].[11] While neither man may have quoted the other in their works, their presence for the other was undeniable. Giacometti's tree sculpture for Beckett's 1961 re-staging of *Waiting for Godot* at the Odéon-Théâtre de l'Europe is a moment of contact which provides just a starting point to understanding the deeper artistic concerns they shared with respect to their own craft over a long period of time. But more than that, it is the relations that can be drawn between their works that reveal a larger, continuous struggle to hold on to and make sense of time and memory from their time to ours. When we read their works today, as Noriyuki does those of Yanaihara, we place ourselves into this struggle and find a way of writing these positions into our own time and place.

But why should we, as readers, feel inclined to find a way of writing these positions of struggle into ours? My response to this question has been that this struggle, for both Beckett and Giacometti, is one firmly rooted in the depiction and perception of human figures, and reading these figures necessarily entails being sensitive to how such fundamental elements as frame, scale and line function in their works. Such a sensitivity in reading necessarily implicates our own positions of seeing, hearing and reading such texts, art works and performances.

As the preceding chapters have shown, the writing of such positions into ours is frequently contorted, leaving us with somewhat ghostly figures. In all the works analyzed, residual figuration results in a partial evacuation of the figure — the gazes of Joe and the late busts are eventually denied, the bodies of Beckett's dramaticules and Giacometti's lithographs are displaced through various types and temporalities of reading, and the radio figures remain to be found in hollows and holes together with Diego. Yet these readings also create or develop different conceptions of the figure and its figuration. Ada, for instance, is a thoroughly ghosted figure, but an analysis of focalization exposes her voice as a type of figuration at once doubly absent and yet aligned with a peculiar experience of ruin. *Paris sans fin*'s plunging woman likewise stretches across as space and stream and body; in traversing the blanks of spatiality and those of temporality (in text, missing text, and lithographic reproduction) she is a figure that, together with that turn of the frontispiece page onto *Paris sans fin* proper, is gap repeated on gap. These creations and developments of new types or parts of figures invariably set off movements of thoughts in the reader's mind enacted way beyond the initial perceptions of the figures as depicted in the works. The words 'metaphor' and 'metonymy' creep up as broad strokes of this movement of thought that conjoins perception and depiction, but what appears to be happening here is a more precise operation of developing, emphasizing or re-inventing a part of the figure that, over the course of the text, is already made partly absent due to residual figuration.

The rhetorical figure prosopopoeia might go some way to connecting the convoluted processes of reading residual figuration with its ghostly residues.[12] Prosopopoeia comes from the Greek word πρόσωπον and refers to the giving of a mask to an entity that is not present (that is it could be fictitious, inanimate or dead); through synecdoche, this has come to mean a giving of face, voice or person to an entity that is not doing the speaking.[13] As a figure regarded by classical rhetoric to belong to the category of *figurae sententiae*, or 'les grandes figures' in French, it was generally regarded as belonging to the highest category of figures that included 'all types of visual representation', and which could very effectively arouse the feelings of its listeners.[14] A rhetorical term which overlapped with prosopopoeia in medieval rhetorical studies was ethopoeia, which has its roots in ἔθος and referred to the bringing out of a character's disposition and moral character.[15] Thus, prosopopoeia has gradually come to be associated with both πρόσωπον and ἔθος, and by implication takes on the figure of representing both appearance and behaviour, external and internal. This is further complicated by its association to *persona*, and through metonymy, to selfhood:

> The Greek term *prosopopoeia* [...] means literally 'making a mask'. The Latin for mask is *persona* and from this word by metonymic extension come all words describing personhood. Cicero uses the word a great deal, and helps it come to mean both a role and a person, such as one's self. To talk of speaking in one's own person is to use a dramatic metaphor: selfhood is always a mask.[16]

To perform prosopopoeia is therefore to give a mask which in turn reveals your own, recalling Wilde's comment in 'The Critic as Artist': 'Man is least himself when he talks in his own person. Give him a mask, and he will tell you the truth'.[17] In classical rhetorical studies, the orator who performs prosopopoeia in speech does so to convince the audience that the conjured entity is present in him and as him.

Take, for example, Mark Anthony's funeral speech in Shakespeare's *Julius Caesar*, III.2: Anthony wins the crowd over by performing the presence of Caesar through his voice (his will) and body (his corpse, or in Appian's version, an image of him in wax), and subsequently insisting that he is no orator and that he merely allowed Caesar's wounds — 'poor poor dumb mouths' — to speak for him.[18] Anthony's prosopopoeia is in fact very complex because he performs it twice without suffering the consequences of letting his identity as orator surface. He first gives his voice to Caesar and lets him speak through the words of his will, and then taking advantage of the crowd's emotion, regains authority of his own voice so as to perform the second prosopopoeia of giving Caesar's dead body the silenced face of the victim. Anthony's prosopopoeia, as befitting of a figure belonging to *figurae sententiae*, is especially effective because it composes not just the name but the personhood of Caesar; Caesar lies there not as a dead body but as a voice unjustified and waiting to be recovered. Prosopopoeia thus conjures visual images by creating whole persons out of a sliding and elision of subjectivities involving the imaginer and imagined, the present and the vanished, the narrator and the character. Here we observe a close relation to the manipulation of deixis and diegesis in the works of Giacometti and Beckett previously discussed. The unflinching gaze of the Lotar busts created through deictic lines that frame the exterior of the eye sockets give the photographer a face beyond physical resemblance; the lines that are spoken by the women of *Come and Go* but are unheard and unread by the audience or the reader give them a voice that exceeds our characterization.

That prosopopoeia necessarily involves the erasure of the orator's identity for the imagined entity constitutes the double bind of prosopopeia, and is what Paul De Man would term the 'self-effacement' and 'defacement' of rhetoric. In 'Autobiography as De-facement', De Man argues for prosopopeia as the trope of autobiography which ultimately reveals the muteness of language.[19] This de-facement occurs when the elision of the orator's identity with the conjured entity is so complete that the listeners take over the prosopopeia and the orator gives over the mask. The transference of prosopopeia reveals the double-bind of the rhetoric to efface and de-face, to de-face because it effaces. This is fully realized, for example, in Gertrude Stein's *The Autobiography of Alice B. Toklas*, where Stein writes as the 'I' and eye of Toklas, and withdraws Toklas's voice precisely by giving her one.[20] This withdrawal happens with the realization that voices can be forced upon and passed over to others — what is 'given' in prosopopoeia are words and their postures, which suggests that personhood is itself a making of its own mask. Prosopopeia gives a mask not only to the absent, but reveals, upon its effacement, the mask that makes up the present:

> The mask is lifelike, but not alive, and because it remains a mask, we can think about putting it on ourselves [...]. We then take over the prosopopoiea. The figure exploits its metonymic basis — it does not in fact create a person, or a mask or face, or even a voice, but rather the words that person is imagined as saying. And in doing this it suggests that it may not be possible to distinguish selfhood from the words we speak. The figure tests the ability of words, sung, spoken, or even simply read, to give the impression that a ghostly presence has been summoned into being.[21]

The turn of the mask thus reveals the *persona* that is inherent in every prosopopeia. De Man further argues that the mask, as a 'harmless veil' of language, ultimately exposes the muteness of the person beneath. The mask of prosopopeia is the linguistic mask that has always defined and thus disfigured all selfhood; it 'deprives and disfigures to the precise extent that it restores'.[22] Therefore, prosopopeia is a figure that gives the absent a voice, a face or a mask, insofar as this giving reveals the giver as the very heart of this lack of πρόσωπον. This is why De Man resists Wordsworth's view of language as an 'ill gift' by virtue of its being a mere 'clothing for thought': prosopopeia reveals, through an inversion of words, that thought is itself a 'succession of voiceless tropes', and remains the only way for one to access the external world.[23]

Clearly a 'succession of voiceless tropes' is a long way from what Cicero or Quintilian conceived in their writings on rhetoric, yet De Man's deconstructionist programme of prosopopoeia provides an interesting entry point to utilizing this rhetorical figure as a tool of comparative reading. Could Beckett's and Giacometti's works be seen to expose such degrees of voicelessness in personhood by way of feigning prosopopoeia itself, that is to repeatedly adopt its main processes — erasure, enactment, elision — while rejecting its eloquence, as conceived in rhetorical studies? If the fulfilment of *inventio*, *dispositio*, *memoria*, *elocutio* and *pronuntiatio* (to which the tropes and figures belong) are needed for the successful use of any figure in oratory, then clearly the works and performances of both Beckett and Giacometti do not strive towards this notion of eloquence. Indeed, if the eloquence of rhetoric is seen first as 'a systematization of natural eloquence' that derives 'originally from life', then the works of Beckett and Giacometti are anti-rhetorical insofar as they are anti-mimetically eloquent.[24] Eloquence, for Beckett and Giacometti, was to be found in the mere attempt to begin seeing and making in the face of what they regarded essentially as various degrees of silence.

It is this anti-rhetorical strand with which the rhetorical pull of reading their works must struggle, and it is into this position of struggle that the work ultimately writes the reader. This position is affective because it is one that gives incompletely, and in its incompleteness leaves the gift in the giving. Take, for instance, the episode of Ada and Henry's 'evocation' 'twenty years earlier' then and transferred back into the mimetic present of the radio play, which hinges on the rhetorical movements of a single word 'don't':

> ADA Don't stand there staring. [...] Don't wet your good boots.
> [*Pause.*]
> HENRY Don't, don't...
> [*Sea suddenly rough.*]
> ADA [*Twenty years earlier, imploring.*] Don't! Don't!
> HENRY [*Ditto, urgent.*] Darling!
> ADA [*Ditto, more feebly.*] Don't!
> HENRY [*Ditto, exultantly.*] Darling!
> [*Rough sea. Ada cries out. Cry and sea amplified, cut off. End of evocation. Pause. Sea calm.* [...]]
> ADA Don't stand there gaping. Sit down.[25]

'Don't' is the word that moves through these lines and gives Henry's and Ada's voices two different faces, each obscuring and speaking for the other, twenty years apart. It transitions from the anaphora (repetition of the same word at the beginning of a sequence of clauses or sentences) in Ada's lines, to the epizeuxis (repetition of a word two or more times with no intervening word) and aposiopesis (breaking off a sentence with its sense incomplete) in Henry's line, onto the ecphonesis (exclamation of extreme emotion) of Ada's cries, builds up through the antanaclasis (using a word twice or more in two or more of its senses) of 'don't implied by the alliterative 'darling', and returns to the anaphora in Ada's line, thus enacting, through a 'prosopopoeia of prosopopoeia' (what I have explicated by way of doubled framing in the previous chapter), the same effect of gradation or climax (similar to anadiplosis, where the last word of a clause or sentence becomes the first in the next, but continued through three or more stages like 'the rungs of a ladder') through repetition.[26] 'Don't' moves through spoken lines, remembered lines and audible lines, but creates its affective meaning only by interacting with the unspoken, forgotten and inaudible lines implied by way of figures that enact rhetorical deviations and turns of thought. The voices and figures here are composed by way of rhetoric but expressed more in terms of what is unsaid, unheard and unseen. Eloquence is here achieved in terms of evoking different degrees of and relations across silence and muteness.

A rhetorical composition, enactment and expression of an unseen 'don't' can be seen, analogously, in Giacometti's works analysed. The rhetorical basis of the sister arts starting from the Renaissance is a vast topic and beyond the scope of this book; however, the writings of Leon Battista Alberti, which form the basis of much of this research, delineate what I think is most insightful for the reading at hand.[27] Alberti defines the aim of painting in three stages: *circumscriptio*, 'where the painter draws the outline of the things to be represented' and is a term in rhetoric referring to 'encircling' and 'definition' in Cicero; *compositio*, 'which unifies the "several surfaces of the object seen"' and is a term in grammar and rhetoric which refers to 'the putting together of the single evolved sentence of period'; and *luminum reception*, which refers to the 'reception of light as it defines "the colours of surfaces"'.[28] As noted by Vickers and Spencer, Alberti comes very close to Quintilian when he draws from the gestures of oratory rather than nature in prescribing that all seven directions of movements (up, down, left, right, going away, coming towards, and going in a circle) should be in a single painting.[29] From this can be drawn Alberti's and various other Renaissance theories of human movement that derive from contraposition, which can in turn be traced to the Greek ἀντίθεσις [antithesis] in which opposites are set against each other.[30]

These very brief insights into the rhetorical theory of composition in Renaissance visual art provide a useful basis for thinking about how the movement in Giacometti's works enacts similar forms of rhetorical theory, but towards a sort of silent, unseen and withdrawn anti-eloquence. The posture of the late Annette bust, for instance, is a leaning forward that is mimetic not of the natural posture of the model but of the movement of cognizing and perceiving something that is distant and blurred. It displaces the rigidity of the bust for the reflexiveness of our position of looking, there reflected and re-created in the face of Annette as a ghostly gaze of looking in and looking back. We have, in this bust, various sets of opposites set against each other, but across depiction and perception: the outward rejection of *contrapposto* in the depicted figure itself — as is the case for all of Giacometti's standing figures — finds its enactment of antithesis in the engagement of our space of looking with that of the figure through manipulations of scale and frame.[31] The bust of Annette moves through such rhetorical thought and re-makes its own face, in turn encircling our own face of looking in a time and space displaced from hers. Here we observe once again a form of anti-eloquence that is achieved by evoking different degrees of and relations across silence and muteness, or what De Man terms 'a mute scene of looking, the mind gazing upon a speaking face'.[32]

The gestural dimension of the human figure that emerges through residual figuration in Beckett's and Giacometti's works could, therefore, be aligned to this incomplete use of prosopopoeia. In this book, I have shown how this is enacted through the palimpsestic making and unmaking of figure and figuration. This mode of reading, residual figuration, shows how degrees of absences and presences thoroughly pervade the works of Beckett and Giacometti through interactions as fundamental — and as complex — as scale, frame and line. But what this reading also uncovers is a lack of pretension on the part of these works to comprehend the unknowns; in the unchanging face of what is 'unmakeable' and 'unseeable', one must continue to struggle, to struggle to make and to make sense of struggling, 'but no masks'.[33] The affective quality of these works thus lies in their utter conviction to struggle better. When we watch a Beckett play or look at a Giacometti lithograph, what we are reading are perhaps Yanaihara's lines passing between the father who has forgotten and the son who tries to remember — a dialogue that is play, and struggle, and which produces a space and time that writes and sustains living.

Notes to the Conclusion

1. Aulus Gellius, *Attic Nights*, I, 399.
2. Noriyuki Kiguchi, *Mon père, Giacometti* (first performed by Akumanoshirushi in Kanagawa Arts Theatre, Kyoto, 2014).
3. See Takeda, '"An Unknown Country"'; Isaku Yanaihara, *Avec Giacometti*, trans. by Véronique Perrin (Paris: Allia, 2014).
4. Isaku Yanaihara, *Dialogues Avec Giacometti*, trans. by Véronique Perrin (Paris: Allia, 2015), p. 5.
5. Ibid.
6. Ibid. pp. 5–6.
7. Isaku Yanaihara, 完本 ジャコメッティ手帖 [The Complete Giacometti Handbook], 2 vols (Tokyo: Misuzu Shobo, 2010), I.
8. See Hohl, *Alberto Giacometti*, p. 172.
9. Isaku Yanaihara, 'Pages de journal', in *Derrière le miroir* (Paris: Aimé Maeght, 1961), pp. 18–26; ジャコメッティ [Giacometti], ed. by Eiji Usami and Akihiko Takeda (Tokyo: Misuzu Shobo, 1996).
10. Yanaihara, 完本 ジャコメッティ手帖 [The Complete Giacometti Handbook], II.
11. Beckett, cited in Knowlson, *Damned to Fame*, p. 720.
12. For prosopopoeia as a tool for reading twentieth-century literary texts and visual art, see for instance: Rochelle Rives, 'Modernist Prosopopoeia: Mina Loy, Gaudier-Brzeska and the

Making of Face', *Journal of Modern Literature*, 34 (2011), 137–59; Joanne Simone Crawford, 'Figuring Death: The Phantom of Presence in Art' (unpublished PhD dissertation, University of Leeds, 2001); Penelope Alice Edith Haynes, 'The Two-faced Trope: Prosopopoeia in Denise Levertov, Margaret Atwood and Louise Glück' (unpublished PhD dissertation, University of Otago, 2011); Nouri Gana, 'The Poetics of Mourning: The Tropologic of Prosopopoeia in Joyce's *The Dead*', *American Imago*, 60 (2003), 159–78.

13. Gavin Alexander, 'Prosopopoeia: The Speaking Figure', in *Renaissance Figures of Speech*, ed. by Sylvia Adamson and others (Cambridge: Cambridge University Press, 2007), pp. 97–114 (pp. 98, 99).
14. Brian Vickers, *In Defence of Rhetoric* (Oxford: Clarendon Press, 1989), pp. 284–85.
15. Alexander, 'Prosopopoeia', p. 99.
16. Ibid. p. 101.
17. Oscar Wilde, 'The Critic as Artist. Part II', in *Intentions* (New York: Brentano, 1905), pp. 151–217 (p. 175).
18. Appian, *The Roman History*, trans. by Horace White, 4 vols, Loeb Classical Library (Cambridge, MA: Harvard University Press, 1912–13), III (*The Civil Wars*), 501; William Shakespeare, *Julius Caesar* [1599], ed. by D. Daniell (London: Thomas Learning, 2005), III.2.218.
19. Paul De Man, 'Autobiography as De-facement', *MLN*, 94 (1979), 919–30.
20. Gertrude Stein, *The Autobiography of Alice B. Toklas* (London: Bodley Head, 1933).
21. Alexander, 'Prosopopoeia', pp. 111–12.
22. De Man, 'Autobiography as De-Facement', p. 930.
23. Ibid. p. 929.
24. Vickers, *In Defence of Rhetoric*, p. 296.
25. Beckett, *Embers*, p. 260.
26. All definitions of rhetorical figures from the index in Vickers, *In Defence of Rhetoric*.
27. See for example Bernard Weinberg, *A History of Literary Criticism in the Italian Renaissance*, 2 vols (Chicago, IL: University of Chicago Press, 1961); John R. Spencer, 'Ut rhetorica pictura: A Study in Quattrocento Theory of Painting', *Journal of the Warburg and Courtauld Institutes*, 20 (1957), 26–44; Michael Baxandall, *Painting and Experience in Fifteenth Century Italy: A Primer in the Social History of Pictorial Style* (Oxford: Oxford University Press, 1988); David Summers, *Michelangelo and the Language of Art* (Princeton, NJ: Princeton University Press, 1981); D. R. Edward Wright, 'Alberti's De Pictura: Its Literary Structure and Purpose', *Journal of the Warburg and Courtauld Institutes* (1984), 52–71.
28. Vickers, *In Defence of Rhetoric*, p. 343.
29. Ibid. p. 349.
30. Ibid., pp. 349, 350; Summers, *Michelangelo and the Language of Art*, p. 76.
31. Hohl, 'Giacometti and His Century', p. 49.
32. Paul De Man, 'Wordsworth and the Victorians', in *The Rhetoric of Romanticism* (New York: Columbia University Press, 2013), pp. 83–92 (p. 90).
33. Beckett, *Play*, p. 307.

BIBLIOGRAPHY

ABBOTT, H. PORTER, 'Tyranny and Theatricality: The Example of Samuel Beckett', *Theatre Journal*, 40 (1988), 77–87

ABRAMSON, ALBERT, *The History of Television, 1942 to 2000* (Jefferson, NC: McFarland, 2002)

ACKERLEY, CHRIS, '"Ever Know What Happened?": Shades and Echoes in Samuel Beckett's Television Plays', *Journal of Beckett Studies*, 18 (2009), 136–64

—— 'Samuel Beckett: The Geometry of the Imagination', in *Samuel Beckett: Debts and Legacies. New Critical Essays*, ed. by Peter Fifield and David Addyman (London: Bloomsbury, 2013), pp. 85–108

Alberto and Annette Giacometti Foundation <http://www.fondation-giacometti.fr>

ALEXANDER, GAVIN, 'Prosopopoeia: The Speaking Figure', in *Renaissance Figures of Speech*, ed. by Sylvia Adamson and others (Cambridge: Cambridge University Press, 2007), pp. 97–114

ALPHEN, ERNST VAN, *Francis Bacon and the Loss of Self* (London: Reaktion books, 1992)

—— 'The Narrative of Perception and the Perception of Narrative', *Poetics Today*, 11 (1990), 483–509

APPIAN, *The Roman History*, trans. by Horace White, 4 vols, Loeb Classical Library (Cambridge, MA: Harvard University Press, 1912–13)

ASHBERY, JOHN, 'Self-portrait in a Convex Mirror', *Poetry*, 124 (1974), 247–61

AULUS GELLIUS, *Attic Nights*, trans. by John Carew Rolfe, 3 vols, Loeb Classical Library (Cambridge, MA: Harvard University Press, 1927)

BAL, MIEKE, *Double Exposures: The Subject of Cultural Analysis* (New York: Routledge, 1996)

—— *Endless Andness: The Politics of Abstraction According to Ann Veronica Janssens* (London: Bloomsbury, 2013)

—— *The Mottled Screen: Reading Proust Visually*, trans. by Anna-Louise Milne (Stanford, CA: Stanford University Press, 1997)

—— *Narratology: Introduction to the Theory of Narrative*, trans. by Christine van Boheeman (Toronto: University of Toronto Press, 2009)

—— *Quoting Caravaggio: Contemporary Art, Preposterous History* (Chicago, IL: University of Chicago Press, 1999)

—— *Reading 'Rembrandt': Beyond the Word-image Opposition* (Amsterdam: Amsterdam University Press, 2006)

—— 'Second-person Narrative', *Paragraph*, 19 (1996), 179–204

BAL, MIEKE, WITH BRYAN GONZALES, eds, *The Practice of Cultural Analysis: Exposing Interdisciplinary Interpretation* (Stanford, CA: Stanford University Press, 1999)

BAL, MIEKE, and JANE E. LEWIN, 'The Narrating and the Focalizing: A Theory of the Agents in Narrative', *Style*, 17 (1983), 234–69

BAL, MIEKE, and SHERRY MARX-MACDONALD, *Travelling Concepts in the Humanities: A Rough Guide* (Toronto: University of Toronto Press, 2002)

BARBER, ELIZABETH WAYLAND, *Women's Work: The First 20,000 Years. Women, Cloth, and Society in Early Times* (New York: W. W. Norton, 1994)

BARTHES, ROLAND, *The Pleasure of the Text*, trans. by Richard Miller (New York: Hill & Wang, 1975)

BAXANDALL, MICHAEL, *Painting and Experience in Fifteenth Century Italy: A Primer in the Social History of Pictorial Style* (Oxford: Oxford University Press, 1988)
BECKETT, SAMUEL, *Les Années Godot: lettres 1941–1956*, ed. by George Craig and others (Paris: Gallimard, 2011)
——*Collected Shorter Prose: 1945–1980* (London: Calder, 1986)
——*The Complete Dramatic Works* (London: Faber & Faber, 2006)
——*Disjecta: Miscellaneous Writings and a Dramatic Fragment* (London: Calder, 1983)
——*Eh Joe*, dir. by Alan Gibson (BBC, 1966)
——*Eh Joe*, dir. by David Clark (University of London Audio-Visual Centre, 1972)
——*How It Is* (London: Calder, 1985)
——*Murphy*, ed. by J. C. C. Mays (London: Faber & Faber, 2009)
——*Quad et autres pièces pour la télévision, suivi de L'Épuisé par Gilles Deleuze*, trans. by Edith Fournier (Paris: Minuit, 1992)
——*Shades: Three Plays by Samuel Beckett*, dir. by Donald McWhinnie and Anthony Page, *The Lively Arts* (BBC, 1977)
——*The Unnamable* (New York: Grove, 1978)
——*Watt* (London: Faber & Faber, 2009)
BECKETT, SAMUEL, and ALAN SCHNEIDER, *No Author Better Served: The Correspondence of Samuel Beckett & Alan Schneider*, ed. by Maurice Harmon (Cambridge, MA: Harvard University Press, 1998)
BEDFORD, CHRISTOPHER, 'Alberto Giacometti', in *The Fran and Ray Stark Collection of 20th-century Sculpture at the J. Paul Getty Museum*, ed. by Antonia Boström (Los Angeles: J. Paul Getty Museum, 2008), pp. 79–81
BENNETT, SUSAN, *Theatre Audiences: A Theory of Production and Reception* (New York: Routledge, 2013)
BENVENISTE, ÉMILE, 'Subjectivity in Language', in *Problems in General Linguistics*, trans. by Mary Elizabeth Meek (Coral Gables, FL: University of Miami Press, 1971), pp. 223–30
BORDWELL, DAVID, JANET STAIGER, and KRISTIN THOMPSON, *The Classical Hollywood Cinema: Film Style & Mode of Production to 1960* (London: Routledge, 1988)
BOSWELL, JAMES, *The Life of Samuel Johnson*, 4 vols (London: Cadell & Davies, 1816)
BRATER, ENOCH, *Beyond Minimalism: Beckett's Late Style in the Theater* (Oxford: Oxford University Press, 1990)
——'Dada, Surrealism, and the Genesis of Not I', *Modern Drama*, 18 (1975), 49–59
——'"A Footnote to *Footfalls*: Footsteps of Infinity on Beckett's Narrow Space', *Comparative Drama*, 12 (1978), 35–41
——'The "I" in Beckett's Not I', *Twentieth-century Literature*, 20 (1974), 189–200
BROWN, LLEWELLYN, *Beckett, Lacan and the Gaze* (Stuttgart: ibidem, 2019)
——*Beckett, Lacan and the Voice* (Stuttgart: ibidem, 2016)
BRYDEN, MARY, 'The Schizoid Space: Beckett, Deleuze, and "L'Épuisé"', *Samuel Beckett Today/ Aujourd'hui*, 5 (1996), 85–94
BRYSON, NORMAN, *Vision and Painting: The Logic of the Gaze* (New Haven, CT: Yale University Press, 1983)
CARRIER, DAVID, *The Aesthete in the City: The Philosophy and Practice of American Abstract Painting in the 1980s* (University Park: Pennsylvania State University Press, 1994)
CHATMAN, SEYMOUR BENJAMIN, *Story and Discourse: Narrative Structure in Fiction and Film* (Ithaca, NY: Cornell University Press, 1980)
CHION, MICHEL, *The Voice in Cinema* (New York: Columbia University Press, 1999)
CONNOR, STEVEN, 'Auf Schwankendem Boden', in *Samuel Beckett, Bruce Nauman* (Vienna: Kunsthalle Wien, 2000), pp. 80–87
——'Shifting Ground <www. stevenconnor.com/beckettnauman/>

——*Beckett, Modernism and the Material Imagination* (Cambridge: Cambridge University Press, 2014)
——*Dumbstruck: A Cultural History of Ventriloquism* (Oxford: Oxford University Press, 2000)
——'"I Switch Off": The Ordeals of Radio', in *Beckett, Modernism and the Material Imagination* (Cambridge: Cambridge University Press, 2014), pp. 65–83
CRAWFORD, JOANNE SIMONE, 'Figuring Death: The Phantom of Presence in Art' (unpublished PhD dissertation, University of Leeds, 2001)
DANIEL, HUGO, 'Samuel Beckett, Alberto Giacometti (Work) in Progress', in *Giacometti Beckett: Rater encore. Rater mieux* (Lyons: Fage, 2020), pp. 19–34
DE MAN, PAUL, 'Autobiography as De-facement', *MLN*, 94 (1979), 919–30
——'Wordsworth and the Victorians', in *The Rhetoric of Romanticism* (New York: Columbia University Press, 2013), pp. 83–92
DELEUZE, GILLES, 'The Exhausted', *SubStance*, 24 (1995), 3–28
DERRIDA, JACQUES, 'The Deaths of Roland Barthes', in *The Work of Mourning*, ed. by Pascale-Anne Brault and Michael Naas (Chicago, IL: University of Chicago Press, 2001), pp. 31–68
——*Memoirs of the Blind: The Self-portrait and Other Ruins*, trans. by Pascale-Anne Brault and Michael Naas (Chicago: University of Chicago Press, 1993)
——*The Truth in Painting*, trans. by Geoff Bennington and Ian McLeod (Chicago, IL: University of Chicago Press, 1987)
——*Writing and Difference*, trans. by Alan Bass (Chicago, IL: University of Chicago Press, 1978)
DOANE, MARY ANN, 'The Close-up: Scale and Detail in the Cinema', *Differences: A Journal of Feminist Cultural Studies*, 14 (2003), 89–111
DOLAR, MLADEN, *A Voice and Nothing More* (Cambridge, MA: MIT Press, 2006)
EASTMAN, MAX, *Colors of Life: Poems and Songs and Sonnets* (New York: Alfred A. Knopf, 1918)
EBITZ, DAVID, 'Review: Vision and Painting: The Logic of the Gaze by Norman Bryson', *The Art Bulletin*, 69 (1987), 155–58
ELAM, KEIR, 'Dead Heads: Damnation-narration in the "Dramaticules"', in *The Cambridge Companion to Beckett*, ed. by John Pilling (Cambridge: Cambridge University Press, 1994), pp. 145–66
ELIOT, T. S., *The Three Voices of Poetry* (Cambridge: Cambridge University Press, 1955)
ELKINS, JAMES, *On Pictures and the Words that Fail Them* (Cambridge: Cambridge University Press, 1998)
ERICKSON, JON, 'The Ghost of the Literary in Recent Theories of Text and Performance', *Theatre Survey*, 47 (2006), 245–51
ESSLIN, MARTIN, 'A Poetry of Moving Images', in *Beckett Translating/ Translating Beckett*, ed. by Alan W. Friedman, Charles Rossman and Dina Sherzer (University Park: Pennsylvannia State University Press, 1987), pp. 65–76
——'Towards the Zero of Language', in *Beckett's Later Fiction and Drama: Texts for Company*, ed. by James Acheson and Arthur Kateryna (New York: St. Martin's, 1987), pp. 35–49
FEHSENFELD, MARTHA, '"Everything Out But the Faces": Beckett's Reshaping of *What Where* for Television', *Modern Drama*, 29 (1986), 229–40
FELDMAN, MATTHEW, 'Beckett, Sartre and Phenomenology', *Limit(e) Beckett* (2010), 1–26
FROST, ROBERT, *Selected Letters of Robert Frost*, ed. by Lawrance R. Thompson (New York: Holt, Rinehart & Winston, 1964)
GANA, NOURI, 'The Poetics of Mourning: The Tropologic of Prosopopoeia in Joyce's *The Dead*', *American Imago*, 60 (2003), 159–78
GARNER, STANTON B., 'Visual Field in Beckett's Late Plays', *Comparative Drama* (1987), 349–73

GENET, JEAN, *L'Atelier d'Alberto Giacometti* (Paris: L'Arbalète, 1963)

GENETTE, GÉRARD, *Narrative Discourse: An Essay in Method*, trans. by Jane E. Lewin (Ithaca, NY: Cornell University Press, 1983)

GETSY, DAVID J., *Body Doubles: Sculpture in Britain, 1877–1905* (New Haven, CT: Yale University Press, 2004)

——'Tactility or Opticality, Henry Moore or David Smith: Herbert Read and Clement Greenberg on the Art of Sculpture, 1956', *Sculpture Journal*, 17 (2008), 75–88

GIACOMETTI, ALBERTO, *Paris sans fin* (Paris: Buchet & Chastel, 2003)

GIDAL, PETER, 'Beckett & Others & Art: A System', *Samuel Beckett Today/ Aujourd'hui*, 11 (2001), 303–14

——*Understanding Beckett: A Study of Monologue and Gesture in the Works of Samuel Beckett* (London: Macmillan, 1986)

GONTARSKI, STANLEY E., 'Revising Himself: Performance as Text in Samuel Beckett's Theatre', *Journal of Modern Literature*, 22 (1998), 131–45

GREENBERG, CLEMENT, *The Collected Essays and Criticism. Volume 3: Affirmations and Refusals, 1950–1956* (Chicago, IL: University of Chicago Press, 1995)

GELLIUS, AULIUS, *Attic Nights*, trans. By John Carew Rolfe, 3 vols, Loeb Classical Library edn (Harvard: Harvard University Press, 1927)

HANSEN, JIM, 'Samuel Beckett's Catastrophe and the Theater of Pure Means', *Contemporary Literature*, 49 (2008), 660–82

HAYNES, PENELOPE ALICE EDITH, 'The Two-faced Trope: Prosopopoeia in Denise Levertov, Margaret Atwood and Louise Glück' (unpublished PhD dissertation, University of Otago, 2011)

HERMAN, DAVID, 'Hypothetical Focalization', *Narrative*, 2 (1994), 230–53

HERREN, GRALEY, *Samuel Beckett's Plays on Film and Television* (New York: Palgrave Macmillan, 2007)

HERRERA DAMAS, SUSANA, 'The Roles of the Narrator in Radio Features', *Recherches en Communication*, 37 (2013), 73–80

HOHL, REINHOLD, *Alberto Giacometti* (New York: H. N. Abrams, 1972)

——'Chronology', in *Alberto Giacometti: Sculpture, Paintings, Drawings*, ed. by Angela Schneider (Munich: Prestel, 2008), pp. 7–43

——'Giacometti and His Century', in *Alberto Giacometti: Sculpture, Paintings, Drawings*, ed. by Angela Schneider (Munich: Prestel, 2008), pp. 45–51

HUMBLE, P. N., 'Review of Vision and Painting: The Logic of the Gaze by Norman Bryson', *Journal of Aesthetics and Art Criticism*, 43 (1984), 219–21

HUNKELER, THOMAS, 'Review of Recent Beckett Criticism in Germany', *Journal of Beckett Studies*, 19 (2010), 273–76

INGOLD, TIM, *Lines: A Brief History* (London: Routledge, 2016)

IPSEN, GESCHE, TIMOTHY MATHEWS and DRAGANA OBRADOVIC, eds, *Provocation and Negotiation: Essays in Contemporary Criticism* (Amsterdam: Rodopi, 2013)

JAHN, MANFRED, 'Windows of Focalization: Deconstructing and Reconstructing a Narratological Concept', *Style*, 30 (1996), 241

JAMES, WILLIAM, *The Principles of Psychology* [1890], 2 vols, (New York: Henry Holt, 1918)

KALB, JONATHAN, 'The Radio and Television Plays, and "Film"', in *The Cambridge Companion to Beckett*, ed. by John Pilling (Cambridge: Cambridge University Press, 1994), pp. 124–44

KANE, BRIAN, *Sound Unseen: Acousmatic Sound in Theory and Practice* (Oxford: Oxford University Press, 2014)

KANT, IMMANUEL, *Der Religion innerhalb der Grenzen der bloßen Vernunft*, 2nd edn (Königsberg: Nicolovius, 1794)

KELLY, JULIA, 'Alberto Giacometti, Michel Leiris and the Myths of Existentialism', in *Giacometti: Critical Essays*, ed. by Peter Read and Julia Kelly (Ashgate: Farnham, 2009), pp. 151–70

KERN, EDITH, *Existential Thought and Fictional Technique: Kierkegaard, Sartre, Beckett* (New Haven. CT: Yale University Press, 1970)

KIGUCHI, NORIYUKI, *Mon père, Giacometti* (first performed by Akumanoshirushi in Kanagawa Arts Theatre, 2014)

KLAVER, ELIZABETH, 'Samuel Beckett's "Ohio Impromptu", "Quad," and "What Where": How It Is in the Matrix of Text and Television', *Contemporary Literature*, 32 (1991), 366–82

KNOWLSON, JAMES, *Damned to Fame: The Life of Samuel Beckett* (New York: Simon & Schuster, 1996)

KNOWLSON, JAMES, ed., *'Happy Days': The Production Notebook of Samuel Beckett* (London: Faber & Faber, 1985)

KRAUSS, ROSALIND E., *The Optical Unconscious* (Cambridge, MA: MIT Press, 1993)

LAUGHLIN, KAREN, '"Looking for Sense...": The Spectator's Response to Beckett's Come and Go', *Modern Drama*, 30 (1987), 137–46

LI, LIN, '"To Narrate" — a Verb in the Middle Voice?: Narrativity and Performance in Samuel Beckett's Krapp's Last Tape and Ohio Impromptu', *Narrative*, 28 (2020), 289–303

LORD, JAMES, *A Giacometti Portrait* (London: Faber & Faber, 1981)

—— *Giacometti: A Biography* (New York: Farrar, Straus & Giroux, 1985)

LUST, HERBERT C., *Giacometti: The Complete Graphics and 15 Drawings* (New York: Tudor, 1970)

LUTOSTAŃSKI, BARTOSZ, 'A Narratology of Radio Drama: Voice, Perspective, Space', *Audionarratology: Interfaces of Sound and Narrative*, 52 (2016), 117

MALKIN, JEANETTE R., *Memory-theater and Postmodern Drama* (Ann Arbor: University of Michigan Press, 1999)

MARSHALL, RICK, *History of Television* (New York: Gallery Books, 1986)

MATHEWS, TIMOTHY, *Alberto Giacometti: The Art of Relation* (London: I. B. Tauris, 2014)

—— 'Walking with Angels in Giacometti and Beckett', *L'Esprit Créateur*, 47 (2007), 29–42

MAZIS, GLEN A., 'Merleau-Ponty's Artist of Depth: Exploring "Eye and Mind" and the Works of Art Chosen by Merleau-Ponty as Preface', *PhaenEx*, 7 (2012), 244–74

MCMULLAN, ANNA, 'Performing Vision(S): Perspectives on Spectatorship in Beckett's Theatre', in *Samuel Beckett: A Casebook*, ed. by Jennifer M. Jeffers and Kimball King (London: Garland, 1998), pp. 133–58

—— 'Samuel Beckett's Scenographic Collaboration with Jocelyn Herbert', *Degrés: revue de synthèse à orientation sémiologique*, 149 (2012), 1–17

—— *Theatre on Trial: Samuel Beckett's Later Drama* (London: Routledge, 2003)

MEGGED, MATTI, *Dialogue in the Void: Beckett and Giacometti* (New York: Lumen Books, 1985)

MERLEAU-PONTY, MAURICE, 'The Intertwining — The Chiasm', in *The Visible and the Invisible*, ed. by Claude Lefort, trans. by Alberto Lingis (Evanston, IL: Northwestern University Press, 1968), pp. 130–55

—— 'Eye and Mind', in *The Merleau-Ponty Aesthetics Reader: Philosophy and Painting*, ed. by Galen A. Johnson (Evanston, IL: Northwestern University Press, 1993), pp. 121–49

MILZ, MANFRED, *Samuel Beckett und Alberto Giacometti: das Innere als Oberfläche. Ein ästhetischer Dialog im Zeichen Schöpferischer Entzweiungsprozesse (1929–1936)* (Würzburg: Königshausen & Neumann, 2006)

MOORJANI, ANGELA, 'Directing or in-Directing Beckett: Or What Is Wrong with Catastrophe's Director?', *Samuel Beckett Today/Aujourd'hui*, 15 (2005), 187–99

NANCY, JEAN-LUC, *The Ground of the Image*, trans. by Jeff Fort (New York: Fordham University Press, 2005)

OLNEY, JAMES, 'Beckett's "Neither" & Giacometti's "Figurine entre deux boîtes qui sont des maisons"', *Daedalus*, 143 (2014), 77–84

——*Memory and Narrative: The Weave of Life-writing* (Chicago, IL: University of Chicago Press, 1998)

OWENS, CRAIG N., 'Applause and Hiss: Implicating the Audience in Samuel Beckett's "Rockaby" and "Catastrophe"', *Journal of the Midwest Modern Language Association*, 36 (2003), 74–81

PEIRCE, CHARLES S., 'Logic as Semiotic: The Theory of Signs', in *Semiotics: An Introductory Anthology*, ed. by R. E. Innis (Bloomington: Indiana University Press, 1985), pp. 1–23

PEPPIATT, MICHAEL, *Alberto Giacometti in Postwar Paris* (New Haven, CT: Yale University Press, 2001)

PINOTTI, ANDREA, 'Soltanto l'essenziale: Beckett e Giacometti', *Quaderni di acme*, 97 (2007), 263–80

POTTS, ALEX, 'Difficult Meanings', *The Burlington Magazine*, 129 (1987), 29–32

——*The Sculptural Imagination: Figurative, Modernist, Minimalist* (New Haven, CT: Yale University Press, 2000)

PRENDEVILLE, BRENDAN, 'Merleau-Ponty, Realism and Painting: Psychophysical Space and the Space of Exchange', *Art History*, 22 (1999), 364–88

PRIETO, ERIC, *Listening In: Music, Mind and the Modernist Narrative* (Lincoln: University of Nebraska Press, 2003)

PRINCE, GERALD, 'A Point of View on Point of View or Refocusing Focalization', in *New Perspectives on Narrative Perspective*, ed. by Willie van Peer and Seymour Chatman (Albany: State University of New York Press, 2001), pp. 43–50

PUCHNER, MARTIN, *Stage Fright: Modernism, Anti-theatricality, and Drama* (Baltimore, MD: Johns Hopkins University Press, 2002)

QUIDEAU, FLORENCE, 'Origins of Modernism in French Romantic Sculpture: David D'Angers, Dantan-Jeune, Daumier and Préault' (unpublished PhD dissertation, Rutgers University, 2011)

RAINFORD, LYDIA, 'How to Read the Image? Beckett's Televisual Memory', in *Literature and Visual Technologies: Writing after Cinema*, ed. by Julian Murphet and Lydia Rainford (Basingstoke: Palgrave Macmillan, 2003), pp. 177–96

READ, HERBERT, *The Art of Sculpture* (New York: Pantheon Books, 1956)

REAVEY, GEORGE, and JAMES KNOWLSON, 'George Reavey and Samuel Beckett's Early Writing: Edited Transcription of an Interview with George Reavey by James Knowlson, 6 August 1971', *Journal of Beckett Studies*, 2 (1977), 9–14

RIVES, ROCHELLE, 'Modernist Prosopopoeia: Mina Loy, Gaudier-Brzeska and the Making of Face', *Journal of Modern Literature*, 34 (2011), 137–59

ROBINSON, FRED MILLER, '"An Art of Superior Tramps": Beckett and Giacometti', *Centennial Review* (1981), 331–44

ROBINSON, JEFFREY CANE, *The Walk: Notes on a Romantic Image* (Rochester: Dalkey Archive Press, 2006)

RODERO, EMMA, 'Stimulating the Imagination in a Radio Story: The Role of Presentation Structure and the Degree of Involvement of the Listener', *Journal of Radio & Audio Media*, 19 (2012), 45–60

RUBIN, EDGAR, 'Figure and Ground', in *Readings in Perception*, ed. by M. Wertheimer and David C. Beardslee (Princeton, NJ: D. Van Nostrand, 1958), pp. 194–203

SARTRE, JEAN-PAUL, *Essays in Aesthetics*, ed. and trans. by Wade Baskin (New York: Open Road Media, 2012)

SCHEIDEGGER, ERNST, DIR., *Alberto Giacometti* (Zurich, 1966)

SCOTT, CLIVE, *Literary Translation and the Rediscovery of Reading* (Cambridge: Cambridge University Press, 2012)

—— *Translating the Perception of Text: Literary Translation and Phenomenology* (Oxford: Legenda, 2012)

SCRIVEN, MICHAEL, *Jean-Paul Sartre: Politics and Culture in Postwar France* (Basingstoke: Palgrave Macmillan, 2016)

SHAKESPEARE, WILLIAM, *Julius Caesar* [1599] (London: Thomas Learning, 2005)

SHEEHAN, PAUL, 'A World Without Monsters: Beckett and the Ethics of Cruelty', in *Beckett and Ethics*, ed. by Russell Smith (London: Continuum, 2008), pp. 86–101

SIMONE, R. THOMAS, '"Faint, Though by No Means Invisible": A Commentary on Beckett's *Footfalls*', *Modern Drama*, 26 (1983), 435–46

SINOIMERI, LEA, '"Close your eyes and listen to it": Schizophonia and Ventriloquism in Beckett's Plays', *Miranda*, 4 (2011) <http://journals.openedition.org/miranda/1924>

SLOTERDIJK, PETER, *Sphären III. Plurale Sphärologie: Schäume* (Frankfurt: Suhrkamp, 2004)

SOLDINI, JEAN, *Alberto Giacometti: la somiglianza introvabile* (Milan: Jaca Book, 1998)

SOLLARS, MICHAEL DAVID, 'Kafkaesque Absurdity in the Aesthetics of Beckett and Giacometti', *Enthymema* (2013), 71–82

SONTAG, SUSAN, *Against Interpretation, and Other Essays* (New York: Farrar, Straus & Giroux, 1966)

SPENCER, JOHN R., 'Ut rhetorica pictura: A Study in Quattrocento Theory of Painting', *Journal of the Warburg and Courtauld Institutes*, 20 (1957), 26–44

STEIN, GERTRUDE, *The Autobiography of Alice B. Toklas* (London: Bodley Head, 1933)

STEVENS, BRETT, 'A Purgatorial Calculus: Beckett's Mathematics in *Quad*', in *A Companion to Samuel Beckett*, ed. by Stanley E. Gontarski (Oxford: Blackwell, 2010), pp. 164–81

SUMMERS, DAVID, *Michelangelo and the Language of Art* (Princeton, NJ: Princeton University Press, 1981)

SYLVESTER, DAVID, *Looking at Giacometti* (London: Pimlico, 1994)

TAKEDA, AKIHIKO, '"An Unknown Country": Isaku Yanaihara's Giacometti Diaries', in *Giacometti: Critical Essays*, ed. by Peter Read and Julie Kelly (Farnham: Ashgate, 2009), pp. 187–207

TATLER, BENJAMIN W., and OTHERS, 'Yarbus, Eye Movements, and Vision', *i-Perception*, 1.1 (2010), 7–27

TOADVINE, THEODORE A. 'The Art of Doubting: Merleau-Ponty and Cézanne', *Philosophy Today*, 41.4 (1997), 545–53

TONNING, ERIK, *Samuel Beckett's Abstract Drama: Works for Stage and Screen, 1962–1985* (Bern: Peter Lang, 2007)

TUBRIDY, DERVAL, 'Vain Reasonings: Not I', in *Samuel Beckett: A Casebook*, ed. by Jennifer M. Jeffers (New York: Routledge, 2012), pp. 111–32

TURNBULL, DAVID, 'String and Stories', in *Encyclopaedia of the History of Science, Technology, and Medicine in Non-western Cultures*, ed. by Helaine Selin (Berlin: Springer, 2008), pp. 2042–44

VICKERS, BRIAN, *In Defence of Rhetoric* (Oxford: Clarendon Press, 1989)

VOIGTS-VIRCHOW, ECKART, 'Exhausted Cameras: Beckett in the Tv-Zoo', *Samuel Beckett: A Casebook*, 25 (1998), 225

WALTON, IZAAK, *Walton's Lives of Dr. John Donne, Sir Henry Wotton, Richard Hooker, George Herbert, and Dr. Robert Sanderson, with Some Account of the Author and His Writings* (Boston: William Veazie, 1865)

WEINBERG, BERNARD, *A History of Literary Criticism in the Italian Renaissance*, 2 vols (Chicago, IL: University of Chicago Press, 1961)

WIESINGER, VÉRONIQUE, *Giacometti Without End* (Hong Kong: Gagosian Gallery, 2014)

WILDE, OSCAR, 'The Critic as Artist. Part II', in *Intentions* (New York: Brentano, 1905), pp. 151–217

WRIGHT, D. R. EDWARD, 'Alberti's De Pictura: Its Literary Structure and Purpose', *Journal of the Warburg and Courtauld Institutes* (1984), 52–71

WUHRMANN, SYLVIE, 'Paris sans fin ou la libération du regard', in Alberto Giacometti, *Paris sans fin* (Paris: Buchet & Chastel, 2003), pp. 7–20

WULF, CATHARINA, *The Savage Eye/ L'Œil fauve: New Essays on Samuel Beckett's Television Plays* (Amsterdam: Rodopi, 1995)

YANAIHARA, ISAKU, *Avec Giacometti*, trans. by Véronique Perrin (Paris: Allia, 2014)

—— *Dialogues avec Giacometti*, trans. by Véronique Perrin (Paris: Éditions Allia, 2015)

—— 'Pages De Journal', in *Derrière le miroir* (Paris: Aimé Maeght, 1961), pp. 18–26

—— ジャコメッティ [Giacometti], ed. by EIJI USAMI and AKIHIKO TAKEDA (Tokyo: Misuzu Shobo, 1996)

—— 完本 ジャコメッティ手帖 [THE COMPLETE GIACOMETTI HANDBOOK], ed. by Akihiko Takeda, 2 vols (Tokyo: Misuzu Shobo, 2010)

YARBUS, ALFRED L., *Eye Movements and Vision*, trans. by Basil Haigh (New York: Springer Science & Business Media, 1967)

ZEIFMAN, HERSCH, 'Come and Go: A Criticule', in *Samuel Beckett: Humanistic Perspectives*, ed. by M. Beja, S. E. Gontarski and P. Astier (Columbus: Ohio State University Press, 1983), pp. 137–44

INDEX

www.ingramcontent.com/pod-product-compliance
Lightning Source LLC
LaVergne TN
LVHW081301100826
845148LV00005B/937

* 9 7 8 1 7 8 1 8 8 6 6 6 3 *